I0008135

Firewalling and Traffic Control: ACLs, Zones and Context-Based Filtering

James Relington

Copyright © 2025 James Relington

All rights reserved

DEDICATION

To those who seek knowledge, inspiration, and new perspectives—
may this book be a companion on your journey, a spark for curiosity,
and a reminder that every page turned is a step toward discovery.

AKNOWLEDGEMENTS

I would like to express my deepest gratitude to everyone who contributed to the creation of this book. To my colleagues and mentors, your insights and expertise have been invaluable. A special thank you to my family and friends for their unwavering support and encouragement throughout this journey.

Introduction to Network Security Principles

In today's hyper-connected world, where data flows continuously across networks spanning homes, corporations, and governments, network security has become a fundamental component of digital infrastructure. The unprecedented growth in digital communication, cloud services, and remote access has expanded the attack surface of modern networks. As a result, the need for strong, adaptable, and intelligent network security strategies is more pressing than ever. At its core, network security aims to protect the integrity, confidentiality, and availability of data as it travels across or resides on a network. Achieving this involves a complex blend of policies, hardware devices, software applications, and trained personnel working together to identify threats, prevent breaches, and respond effectively when incidents occur.

The basic principles of network security revolve around the classic CIA triad: confidentiality, integrity, and availability. Confidentiality ensures that sensitive data is accessed only by authorized individuals. This includes using encryption to protect data in transit and at rest, as well as employing access controls to regulate who can see or use particular information. Integrity focuses on ensuring that data is not altered or tampered with, either maliciously or accidentally. This is enforced through hashing, checksums, digital signatures, and other verification methods. Availability refers to ensuring that the network and its resources are accessible when needed. Denial-of-service attacks and system failures can disrupt availability, so redundancy, load balancing, and failover mechanisms are employed to mitigate such risks.

While these principles provide the foundation, the actual implementation of network security is multifaceted and dynamic. One of the first steps in securing a network is to establish a secure perimeter. Firewalls, intrusion detection and prevention systems (IDS/IPS), and network segmentation help monitor and control the flow of traffic entering and exiting the network. Firewalls, for example, act as gatekeepers that allow or block traffic based on predefined rules. They enforce security policies by examining packet headers, analyzing protocols, and, in more advanced models, inspecting the actual content of traffic to detect threats.

However, perimeter defense is no longer sufficient in isolation. With the rise of mobile devices, cloud computing, and remote work, traditional network boundaries have blurred. Consequently, modern network security must also focus on internal threats and adopt a defense-in-depth approach. This involves layering multiple security controls throughout the network to create redundancy and reduce the likelihood of a successful breach. Techniques such as network segmentation, which divides the network into isolated zones, help limit the spread of malware or unauthorized access. Access control lists (ACLs), authentication systems, and context-aware policies further enforce who can access what resources and under what conditions.

User awareness and education are also vital components of effective network security. No matter how sophisticated the technology is, it can be undermined by human error or negligence. Social engineering attacks, such as phishing, exploit the human element to gain access to secured systems. Training users to recognize suspicious emails, use strong passwords, and follow security protocols can significantly reduce these risks. Furthermore, security policies must be clearly defined, communicated, and enforced across the organization. Policies should address acceptable use, data handling, incident response, and regular auditing procedures to ensure ongoing compliance and accountability.

Another critical principle in network security is the concept of least privilege. This means that users and systems are granted only the minimum access necessary to perform their tasks. By limiting permissions, organizations can reduce the potential damage if an account is compromised. Role-based access control (RBAC) and attribute-based access control (ABAC) models are commonly used to enforce this principle, ensuring that permissions are aligned with job functions and contextual factors like time, location, or device type.

Monitoring and logging are equally important in maintaining network security. Security teams need visibility into network activities to detect anomalies, investigate incidents, and respond swiftly. Logs from firewalls, routers, servers, and endpoints provide valuable data for identifying patterns and pinpointing suspicious behavior. Security information and event management (SIEM) systems aggregate and analyze this data in real time, using advanced analytics and machine learning to highlight potential threats before they cause significant damage.

The landscape of network threats is constantly evolving. Attackers employ increasingly sophisticated methods such as zero-day exploits, polymorphic malware, and advanced persistent threats (APTs) to bypass traditional defenses. To counter this, organizations must adopt a proactive and adaptive mindset. Threat intelligence, which involves collecting and analyzing data about current and emerging threats, can help inform defensive strategies and prioritize security investments. Regular vulnerability assessments and penetration testing also help uncover weaknesses in the network before attackers can exploit them.

As networks grow in complexity, the need for automation and orchestration in security becomes evident. Manual configurations and responses are no longer practical for large-scale environments. Security tools must integrate seamlessly and respond automatically to certain types of threats. For example, if an intrusion detection system identifies unusual behavior, it can trigger automated rules in a firewall to block the offending IP address immediately. This type of integrated response minimizes response time and reduces human error.

Ultimately, the principles of network security must be tailored to the unique needs, risks, and operational realities of each organization.

There is no one-size-fits-all solution. A robust network security strategy must be flexible, scalable, and continually evolving. It requires not only the right technology but also a commitment to a security-first culture throughout the organization. By understanding and applying the foundational principles of network security, organizations can build resilient infrastructures capable of withstanding the challenges of today and the uncertainties of tomorrow.

The Role of Firewalls in Modern Networks

Firewalls have become a cornerstone of modern network security architecture. As the first line of defense against unauthorized access and malicious traffic, firewalls are responsible for controlling the flow of data between networks with different trust levels, such as the public internet and a private corporate intranet. Their primary role is to enforce security policies by filtering incoming and outgoing network traffic based on predefined rules. Over time, firewalls have evolved from simple packet filters into sophisticated security systems capable of stateful inspection, deep packet analysis, and even application-level control. This evolution reflects the increasing complexity of threats targeting modern digital environments and the necessity for more advanced mechanisms to counter them.

In traditional network setups, the firewall sits at the perimeter, guarding the boundary between the internal network and external sources. This perimeter-focused model was based on the assumption that threats originate outside the organization and that internal users are trustworthy. While this was effective in the early days of networking, the rise of cloud computing, remote work, mobile devices, and sophisticated cyberattacks has rendered the old assumptions obsolete. Modern networks no longer have clear perimeters. Data flows across various endpoints, devices, and cloud services, often bypassing traditional security boundaries. As a result, firewalls have had to adapt, becoming more integrated and distributed across the network.

Modern firewalls do more than just block or allow traffic based on IP addresses and port numbers. They perform stateful inspection, which means they monitor the state of active connections and make decisions based on the context of the traffic. This enables them to track sessions and ensure that incoming packets are legitimate responses to requests initiated from within the network. By keeping a state table of active sessions, firewalls can better detect anomalies, prevent spoofed packets, and stop unauthorized data flows that would bypass simple stateless filtering.

Beyond stateful inspection, next-generation firewalls (NGFWs) provide even deeper visibility and control. They incorporate features such as intrusion prevention systems (IPS), deep packet inspection (DPI), and application awareness. This allows them to identify and control traffic at the application layer, regardless of the port or protocol used. For example, a next-generation firewall can differentiate between normal web traffic and encrypted command-and-control communications hidden within HTTPS sessions. It can block access to specific applications or services and enforce policies based on user identity, device type, or behavior. This level of granular control is essential in modern environments where users and devices are constantly moving and accessing a wide array of cloud-based resources.

Firewalls also play a critical role in implementing network segmentation. By dividing the network into distinct zones, firewalls control the flow of traffic between segments and prevent lateral movement by attackers. This is especially important in environments that host sensitive data or critical infrastructure. For instance, a company may segment its financial systems from its guest Wi-Fi and development environments, allowing access only to authorized users and blocking unnecessary traffic between zones. This limits the potential damage of a breach and makes it easier to detect and respond to suspicious activity.

In addition to their security benefits, firewalls provide valuable logging and auditing capabilities. Every decision they make—whether to allow, block, or inspect traffic—is recorded in detailed logs. These logs are indispensable for network administrators, providing insights into network usage, identifying policy violations, and helping to trace the origins of security incidents. When integrated with security information and event management (SIEM) systems, firewall logs contribute to a comprehensive view of an organization's security posture and enable faster, more effective incident response.

The role of firewalls is also increasingly tied to compliance. Regulations such as GDPR, HIPAA, PCI-DSS, and others require organizations to implement specific safeguards for protecting data and systems. Firewalls, when properly configured and managed, help meet these requirements by enforcing access controls, protecting sensitive information, and providing traceable records of network activity. Failing to properly implement and maintain firewall policies can lead to regulatory penalties, reputational damage, and exposure to avoidable risks.

Cloud environments present unique challenges and opportunities for firewall deployment. Traditional hardware firewalls cannot protect workloads that exist entirely within virtual networks or span multiple geographic regions in a public cloud. As a response, cloud providers and third-party vendors offer virtual firewalls and firewall-as-a-service (FWaaS) solutions that are designed specifically for cloud-native infrastructure. These services provide dynamic scalability, centralized management, and integration with cloud-native security tools. They support automation and orchestration, allowing organizations to deploy consistent security policies across hybrid and multi-cloud environments without sacrificing flexibility.

Moreover, firewalls are now integral to zero trust architecture, a modern security model that assumes no implicit trust based on network location. In a zero trust environment, every request for access is verified explicitly, and microsegmentation is employed to limit access to the smallest possible perimeter. Firewalls help enforce zero trust principles by controlling access between workloads, users, and services at a very granular level. Policies are defined based on identities and context rather than IP addresses alone, making firewalls a crucial enforcement point in this distributed security model.

Despite their critical importance, firewalls are not a silver bullet. They must be part of a layered defense strategy that includes endpoint protection, intrusion detection, user training, and continuous monitoring. Misconfigurations, outdated firmware, or overly permissive rules can all undermine the effectiveness of a firewall.

Therefore, ongoing management, regular audits, and policy reviews are essential to ensure firewalls continue to function as intended and adapt to changes in the network landscape.

The role of firewalls in modern networks is more significant than ever. They have evolved from simple filtering devices into comprehensive security platforms capable of addressing a wide range of threats and operational challenges. Their functions have expanded to include application awareness, user identification, threat prevention, and cloud integration. As organizations embrace digital transformation, the demand for smarter, more adaptive firewall technologies will only continue to grow. Firewalls, when used correctly, provide essential visibility, control, and protection in an ever-changing threat landscape, reinforcing their position as a foundational element of modern cybersecurity strategy.

Types of Firewalls and Their Evolution

The development of firewall technology has mirrored the evolution of networking itself, growing in complexity and functionality in response to an ever-changing threat landscape. In its earliest form, a firewall was a simple mechanism designed to filter traffic based on predefined rules, typically examining IP addresses, ports, and protocols. These early firewalls operated at the network layer and provided basic security by permitting or denying packets according to static rule sets. As threats became more sophisticated and the nature of network communication changed, firewalls had to evolve to offer deeper inspection, more contextual awareness, and dynamic adaptability. Understanding the different types of firewalls and how they have evolved is critical for designing effective security architectures in modern networks.

The earliest and simplest type of firewall is the packet-filtering firewall. This type of firewall examines packets at the network layer (Layer 3) and transport layer (Layer 4) of the OSI model. It uses access control lists to make decisions based on IP addresses, protocol types, and port numbers. Packet-filtering firewalls are fast and efficient because they do not examine the payload or keep track of the state of connections. However, they are also limited in their capabilities, as they lack the ability to understand the context of traffic or distinguish between legitimate and malicious behavior beyond basic parameters. This made them vulnerable to spoofing, session hijacking, and other more advanced attacks.

To address these shortcomings, stateful inspection firewalls were developed. Also known as dynamic packet-filtering firewalls, these systems track the state of active connections and make filtering decisions based on the context of traffic. They understand whether a packet is part of an existing connection or an attempt to initiate a new one. By maintaining a state table, they can verify that incoming packets are valid responses to legitimate requests from within the network. This approach significantly enhanced the security capabilities of firewalls, allowing them to block unsolicited inbound traffic and better resist spoofing and denial-of-service attacks. Stateful firewalls became the standard for enterprise networks during the late 1990s and early 2000s.

As application usage over the internet exploded, particularly with the advent of web-based services, attackers began hiding malicious activity inside legitimate protocols and ports. To combat this, firewalls evolved again, giving rise to application-layer firewalls. These firewalls operate at Layer 7 of the OSI model and are capable of inspecting the actual content of traffic, not just its headers. They can detect and control applications such as web browsers, email clients, file-sharing services, and even specific behaviors within applications. This deeper inspection enables more precise control over what types of traffic are allowed, helping to prevent the exploitation of application-level vulnerabilities. Application-layer firewalls also facilitate data loss prevention by examining payloads for sensitive information such as credit card numbers or personal data.

The introduction of next-generation firewalls (NGFWs) marked another major leap forward in firewall technology. These devices combine the functions of packet filtering, stateful inspection, and application awareness with advanced threat detection and prevention features. NGFWs incorporate intrusion prevention systems, antivirus scanning, sandboxing, and behavioral analytics into a single platform. They are capable of enforcing policies based on user identity, device type, time of day, and even geolocation. By integrating with directory services like Active Directory, NGFWs can apply role-based access controls and log activities tied to specific users. This comprehensive approach allows organizations to create granular, context-aware policies that are more effective at detecting and mitigating modern threats.

Virtual firewalls have emerged to meet the needs of cloud computing and virtualization. Traditional hardware-based firewalls are not well-suited for environments where workloads are dynamically created and migrated across physical boundaries. Virtual firewalls are software-based solutions that can be deployed within virtual machines, containers, or cloud instances. They offer the same capabilities as physical firewalls but with the added flexibility and scalability required for cloud-native infrastructures. These firewalls can enforce east-west traffic control within data centers, ensuring that traffic between virtual machines or containers is inspected and secured. They also integrate with orchestration tools and cloud management platforms, allowing for automated policy deployment and compliance across multi-cloud environments.

With the rise of distributed networks and the proliferation of remote work, firewall functionality has further extended into the realm of Firewall-as-a-Service (FWaaS). This cloud-delivered model provides centralized firewall capabilities through a subscription service, eliminating the need for on-premises hardware. FWaaS offers consistent policy enforcement across all users and devices, regardless of their physical location. It supports secure web gateways, DNS filtering, and identity-based access controls. Because it is cloud-native, FWaaS scales easily to meet changing demand and is often integrated with broader secure access service edge (SASE) solutions that include SD-WAN, zero trust network access, and data protection services.

Another significant innovation in firewall technology is the use of machine learning and artificial intelligence to enhance detection and response. Modern firewalls leverage these technologies to identify patterns, detect anomalies, and adapt to emerging threats. Rather than relying solely on static rules or known signatures, intelligent firewalls can learn from network behavior, flag suspicious activity, and take proactive measures such as isolating devices or blocking traffic in real time. This level of automation and insight is essential for managing security in large-scale, high-velocity environments where human administrators cannot manually evaluate every event.

Despite their advancements, firewalls are not a one-size-fits-all solution. Different environments and use cases call for different types of firewalls or combinations thereof. A small business may rely on a unified threat management device that includes firewall functions alongside antivirus and content filtering, while a large enterprise might deploy multiple tiers of NGFWs, virtual firewalls, and cloud-based solutions. The evolution of firewalls reflects the necessity to respond to increasingly sophisticated and persistent threats with equally sophisticated and adaptive defenses.

As networks continue to evolve, particularly with the adoption of technologies like the Internet of Things, 5G, and edge computing, firewalls will remain a central part of the security infrastructure. They will need to continue adapting, becoming more decentralized, intelligent, and integrated with other security tools. The concept of what a firewall is will keep expanding, but its core mission—to protect and control the flow of data between trusted and untrusted zones—will remain unchanged. Firewalls have transitioned from simple gatekeepers to complex guardians of digital communication, and their journey is far from over.

Packet Filtering Fundamentals

Packet filtering is one of the foundational concepts in network security and serves as the basis for how early firewalls operated. It involves inspecting each packet of data that enters or leaves a network and making a decision to either allow or block it based on a set of predefined rules. These rules typically evaluate information contained in the packet headers, such as source and destination IP addresses, source and destination port numbers, and the protocol being used, like TCP, UDP, or ICMP. This form of filtering operates primarily at the network and transport layers of the OSI model, which correspond to Layers 3 and 4, respectively. Although simple in design, packet filtering remains a relevant and essential tool in network security, especially when used in conjunction with more advanced methods.

The concept of a packet is central to understanding how filtering works. In the context of IP networking, data is broken down into small units called packets before being transmitted across a network. Each packet contains two primary parts: the header and the payload. The header includes metadata such as addressing information, sequence numbers, and control flags, while the payload carries the actual data being transmitted. Packet filtering focuses exclusively on the information in the header, ignoring the contents of the payload. This makes the process faster and less resource-intensive but also limits its ability to detect threats that are embedded within the data itself.

At its most basic level, a packet-filtering firewall uses access control lists to determine whether a packet should be permitted or denied. These access control rules are written to match certain criteria. For example, a rule might permit all traffic from a trusted internal IP address to a specific port on a web server, while denying any inbound traffic from unknown or untrusted external sources. Because each rule is applied independently to individual packets, the firewall does not maintain any awareness of connection state or the sequence of packets. As a result, packet filtering is considered stateless, meaning it treats every packet as a standalone unit without context.

This stateless nature introduces both strengths and limitations. One of the primary advantages of packet filtering is speed. Because it involves a simple rule check based on header fields, it can be performed very quickly, even on high-volume networks. This makes it suitable for use in environments where performance is critical and security requirements are basic. It also has a low resource footprint, meaning it can be deployed on devices with limited processing power or memory. Furthermore, its simplicity makes it relatively easy to configure and understand, which is beneficial in smaller networks or for administrators with limited experience.

However, these same characteristics also create weaknesses. Since packet filtering lacks awareness of session state, it cannot distinguish between legitimate responses to internal requests and unsolicited inbound packets that may be part of an attack. For example, if an internal client initiates a connection to a web server, the return traffic must be allowed back in. A stateless firewall cannot track this behavior and must rely on additional rules to permit the return traffic, potentially exposing the network to spoofed packets that appear to be legitimate. It also cannot detect application-layer attacks, such as those targeting vulnerabilities in HTTP or SMTP protocols, because it does not examine payloads or application behavior.

To manage traffic effectively with packet filtering, administrators must carefully construct and order their rules. Since rules are typically processed in a top-down fashion, the order in which they are written can have a significant impact on firewall behavior. A more general rule placed above a more specific one may inadvertently allow or block traffic in ways that contradict the administrator's intent. This requires careful planning, regular auditing, and a solid understanding of the network's structure and traffic patterns. Any misconfiguration or oversight in rule logic can create security gaps or disrupt legitimate communication.

Another challenge with packet filtering is its limited ability to handle dynamic or encrypted traffic. Many modern applications use dynamic ports or encrypt their data to enhance security. Packet filters that rely solely on fixed port numbers and protocol types may struggle to identify and manage such traffic. This is particularly true in environments with heavy use of VPNs, SSL/TLS encryption, or peer-to-peer applications that operate on unpredictable port ranges. In these cases, more sophisticated inspection methods, such as stateful or deep packet inspection, may be required to achieve the necessary level of control.

Despite its limitations, packet filtering still has an important role to play in layered security architectures. It can be used as a first line of defense, providing a fast and efficient way to block clearly malicious or unnecessary traffic at the perimeter. It can also be employed within internal network segments to restrict traffic between departments or systems, reducing the potential for lateral movement by attackers. When used in conjunction with stateful inspection, intrusion detection systems, and endpoint protection, packet filtering contributes to a broader defense-in-depth strategy that addresses both known and unknown threats.

Moreover, packet filtering has been extended and enhanced over time to support additional features. For instance, some modern packet filters support time-based rules that allow traffic only during specific hours or under specific conditions. Others can log and alert administrators about rule matches, providing visibility into traffic patterns and potential policy violations. These enhancements help bridge the gap between basic filtering and more advanced security needs, making packet filtering a flexible and enduring tool in the network security toolkit.

The underlying principles of packet filtering continue to inform the design of more complex firewalls and security appliances. Even in next-generation systems, packet-level analysis is often the first step before deeper inspection and policy enforcement. Understanding how packet filtering works, its strengths and weaknesses, and how it integrates into larger security frameworks is essential for any network professional. While the threats and technologies have changed dramatically since the early days of networking, the core logic of examining packets and making decisions based on policy remains a fundamental building block of secure communication.

Understanding Access Control Lists (ACLs)

Access Control Lists, commonly referred to as ACLs, are a fundamental tool used in computer networks to control the flow of traffic and enforce security policies. At their core, ACLs provide a method of defining what types of traffic are allowed to enter or exit a network device based on various attributes such as IP addresses, protocols, and ports. ACLs are configured on routers, switches, and firewalls to permit or deny packets, enabling administrators to establish rules that govern access between different network segments. Their role in shaping traffic and enforcing access restrictions makes them essential components of both security frameworks and traffic optimization strategies.

An ACL operates by examining each packet and matching it against a series of rules written by the network administrator. These rules are processed in a sequential manner, from top to bottom, until a match is found. Once a rule matches the packet's characteristics, the associated action—typically permit or deny—is applied, and no further rules are evaluated. If no match is found by the time the end of the list is reached, a default action, usually to deny the packet, is enforced. This sequential processing highlights the importance of rule order within an ACL, as placing a broad rule before a more specific one can unintentionally override the desired behavior.

There are two primary types of ACLs: standard and extended. Standard ACLs are relatively simple and focus only on the source IP address of the traffic. They allow administrators to permit or deny traffic based solely on where it comes from, making them easier to configure but also more limited in precision. Extended ACLs, on the other hand, provide much more control by allowing filtering based on both source and destination IP addresses, as well as the protocol and even specific port numbers. This added granularity enables more targeted security policies, such as permitting HTTP traffic from a particular network while denying FTP traffic from another.

When implementing ACLs, it is critical to consider the direction in which the list is applied. ACLs can be applied in the inbound or outbound direction on an interface. An inbound ACL filters traffic as it arrives on an interface before it is processed by the router or firewall, whereas an outbound ACL filters traffic after it has been processed and is about to be sent out of an interface. Choosing the appropriate direction depends on the specific goals of the rule. For instance, to prevent certain users from accessing external websites, an outbound ACL might be used to deny HTTP traffic from their IP addresses. Conversely, to protect internal servers from unauthorized access, an inbound ACL could be applied to block incoming traffic from unknown sources.

Wildcard masks are a distinctive feature used in ACLs to specify ranges of IP addresses. Unlike subnet masks that define network and host portions, wildcard masks are used to identify which bits in the IP address should be checked and which should be ignored. This allows for flexible matching of address ranges. For example, a wildcard mask can be used to match all hosts within a particular subnet or even to specify every other host in a given range. Mastery of wildcard mask notation is essential for writing efficient and accurate ACL entries, and mistakes in wildcard calculations can result in unintended access being granted or legitimate traffic being blocked.

ACLs are not only used for security purposes but also for traffic shaping and network performance optimization. For example, they can be integrated with Quality of Service policies to classify traffic and ensure that high-priority data, such as voice or video, receives the necessary bandwidth. ACLs can also be employed to manage routing updates by filtering which routing advertisements are accepted or sent to neighboring routers. This capability is especially useful in large or multi-vendor environments where precise control over routing behavior is necessary to maintain network stability.

One of the challenges with ACLs is managing complexity as the network grows. Large ACLs with many rules can become difficult to read and maintain, especially when multiple administrators are involved in their creation and editing. Inconsistent naming conventions, duplicate entries, and poorly documented rules can lead to confusion and misconfigurations. To address this, named ACLs were introduced, allowing administrators to assign descriptive names to ACLs rather than relying on numeric identifiers. This small but significant improvement enhances readability and manageability, particularly in enterprise-scale deployments.

Another variation that adds functionality is the use of dynamic ACLs, which offer time-based or authentication-based control over access. With dynamic ACLs, access permissions can be granted temporarily to authenticated users or restricted to certain time periods, providing flexibility in environments where access requirements change frequently. This feature is particularly useful in organizations with mobile or temporary workers, where granting permanent access would be too permissive but denying access entirely would hinder productivity.

Despite their power and flexibility, ACLs must be used thoughtfully. Over-reliance on ACLs without a broader security strategy can create blind spots. For instance, while ACLs can block traffic based on IP addresses, they cannot inspect encrypted payloads or recognize complex attack patterns hidden in application-layer traffic. Therefore, they should be integrated into a multi-layered defense strategy that includes firewalls, intrusion prevention systems, endpoint security, and monitoring tools. When used in combination with these technologies, ACLs enhance the overall security posture by providing a first line of defense and enforcing consistent traffic policies across the network.

ACLs also play a key role in compliance. Regulatory standards often require organizations to control access to sensitive data and critical systems. Properly configured ACLs help demonstrate that access to systems and data is restricted to authorized users and that unnecessary access paths are blocked. They provide auditability, as changes to ACLs can be tracked and reviewed, ensuring that access rules align with organizational policies and compliance requirements.

Ultimately, understanding how ACLs work, how to write them effectively, and how to apply them strategically is essential for any network administrator or security professional. While their syntax and operation may seem straightforward at first glance, their true value lies in the precision and control they offer when managing network access. When configured correctly and used in the appropriate context, ACLs provide a powerful means of enforcing security, optimizing traffic, and maintaining a well-structured and resilient network environment.

Standard vs Extended ACLs

Access Control Lists, or ACLs, are essential components of network security, enabling administrators to define which traffic is permitted or denied through network devices such as routers and firewalls. Among the different types of ACLs, standard and extended ACLs represent two fundamental approaches to traffic filtering. While both serve the primary function of controlling data flow, they differ significantly in terms of granularity, flexibility, and application. Understanding the distinctions between standard and extended ACLs is crucial for designing effective access control strategies that align with the needs of modern networks.

Standard ACLs are the simplest form of access control lists. Their primary function is to permit or deny traffic based solely on the source IP address of packets. This simplicity makes them easy to configure and manage, particularly in smaller networks or in environments where broad access rules are sufficient. When a standard ACL is applied to a router interface, it evaluates whether the source IP address of a packet matches any of the rules defined in the ACL. If a match is found, the associated action is taken, either allowing the packet to pass or discarding it. If no match is found, the implicit deny rule at the end of the list drops the packet.

This basic functionality is advantageous in scenarios where the objective is to filter entire networks or hosts without regard for specific services or destinations. For example, a standard ACL might be used to block all traffic from a particular subnet from accessing any part of the network. Because it does not consider destination addresses or protocol types, it is straightforward but also limited in precision. In environments where finer control is needed, such as allowing certain types of traffic while blocking others, standard ACLs may prove inadequate.

Extended ACLs, by contrast, provide a much greater degree of control over traffic. These ACLs evaluate not only the source IP address but also the destination IP address, the protocol in use, and, in the case of TCP or UDP traffic, the source and destination port numbers. This means that an extended ACL can be configured to allow or block specific services, such as HTTP or FTP, between particular hosts or subnets. For instance, it is possible to permit HTTPS traffic from a defined internal range to an external web server while blocking all other traffic to that destination. This level of specificity is essential in modern networks, where services must be exposed in a controlled and secure manner.

The additional granularity of extended ACLs makes them particularly useful in environments where multiple applications share the same network infrastructure. By defining rules based on protocol and port numbers, administrators can isolate application traffic, prioritize essential services, and minimize the exposure of sensitive systems to unauthorized access. This also enables the creation of policy-based access control, where access decisions are based on the type of service being accessed rather than simply the identity of the device initiating the connection.

However, the increased functionality of extended ACLs comes with added complexity. Writing and managing extended ACLs requires a deeper understanding of networking protocols, port usage, and traffic flows. Misconfigurations can lead to unintended consequences, such as legitimate traffic being blocked or insecure services being inadvertently allowed. Furthermore, as the number of rules grows, extended ACLs can become difficult to audit and troubleshoot without a well-documented and consistent naming and numbering scheme.

Placement of ACLs within the network architecture is another area where the distinction between standard and extended ACLs becomes important. Because standard ACLs filter traffic based only on the source IP address, they are most effectively placed as close as possible to the destination. This prevents legitimate traffic from being denied too early in its path, especially when multiple destinations share the same source. Extended ACLs, on the other hand, can be placed closer to the source of traffic because they take both source and destination information into account. This allows administrators to filter undesired traffic before it traverses the network, conserving bandwidth and reducing potential exposure to threats.

When applying either type of ACL, careful planning is essential. Rules are processed in order from top to bottom, and the first matching rule dictates the action taken. This means that the order in which rules are written can dramatically affect their behavior. For both standard and extended ACLs, it is a best practice to place more specific rules higher in the list and broader, more general rules lower down. This ensures that exceptions are evaluated before general cases and minimizes the risk of inadvertently blocking critical traffic.

Named ACLs are another feature that can apply to both standard and extended types. Instead of using numeric identifiers, named ACLs allow administrators to assign meaningful names to their ACL configurations. This improves readability and maintainability, especially in environments where multiple ACLs are in use. Named ACLs also support advanced features like sequence numbers, which allow individual rules to be added, removed, or modified without rewriting the entire list.

In real-world networks, the choice between standard and extended ACLs depends largely on the specific security and traffic management objectives. For simpler access policies, where only the source of traffic needs to be considered, standard ACLs provide a lightweight and effective solution. In contrast, extended ACLs are better suited for environments that require detailed control over traffic types, destinations, and services. They provide the flexibility necessary to enforce least privilege principles, control access to critical applications, and limit the exposure of internal systems to external threats.

As networks become more complex and as security demands increase, extended ACLs have become more prevalent. Their ability to differentiate traffic based on protocol and port is essential in a world where cyber threats often masquerade as normal application traffic. However, both types of ACLs continue to serve vital roles. When used appropriately and configured with care, they contribute significantly to a secure, efficient, and well-organized network. Administrators must be familiar with the capabilities and limitations of both standard and extended ACLs to apply them effectively in any given scenario, ensuring that the network remains both accessible to legitimate users and protected from unauthorized activity.

Creating and Applying ACLs

Creating and applying Access Control Lists, or ACLs, is a critical skill in network administration that directly affects the security, accessibility, and performance of a network. ACLs are used to define traffic filtering rules that determine which packets are allowed or denied as they pass through network devices like routers, switches, and firewalls. By specifying conditions based on attributes such as IP addresses, protocols, and port numbers, ACLs enforce access policies that help protect the network from unauthorized use, malicious traffic, and unintended data exposure. The process of creating and applying ACLs requires a thoughtful approach, a solid understanding of network architecture, and careful attention to detail to avoid disrupting legitimate communication while effectively blocking threats.

The first step in creating an ACL is defining its purpose. Whether the goal is to restrict access to a specific server, limit web browsing from a group of users, or permit only secure protocols, having a clear objective is essential. Without a defined goal, it becomes easy to create rules that are either too broad or too narrow, resulting in excessive access or unnecessary blockages. Understanding the traffic flow, the devices involved, and the services in use will help shape the design of the ACL and ensure that it aligns with the overall network policy.

Once the objective is clear, the next phase involves writing the actual rules that make up the ACL. These rules are built using specific syntax that depends on the device's operating system, but the logic remains consistent across platforms. For standard ACLs, rules are created using only the source IP address as the condition. For example, a rule might deny all traffic originating from a particular subnet. Extended ACLs, which are more granular, allow the inclusion of destination IP addresses, protocols like TCP or UDP, and even specific ports such as HTTP port 80 or SSH port 22. These additional parameters enable much finer control and allow administrators to create policies that reflect real-world requirements more closely.

Creating effective ACL rules means understanding how to use wildcard masks to define IP ranges. A wildcard mask tells the device which parts of an IP address to consider in the match and which parts to ignore. Unlike subnet masks, which define network boundaries, wildcard masks are used in ACLs to specify sets of addresses in a flexible and efficient way. For instance, a wildcard mask of 0.0.0.255 applied to an IP address would match all hosts in the last octet, allowing a rule to apply to an entire range rather than a single address. Mastery of wildcard logic is essential for writing ACLs that are both accurate and efficient.

Rule order is another critical factor in the success of an ACL. ACLs are processed sequentially from the top of the list to the bottom, and the first rule that matches a packet determines its fate. If a rule at the top of the list permits a certain kind of traffic, that packet is allowed through, and the rest of the rules are ignored. This means that more specific rules should generally come before more general ones to avoid unintentional matches. For example, if an administrator wants to deny access to one particular host but allow the rest of the network, the deny rule must come first, followed by the permit rule for the larger range. Misordering rules is a common mistake that can lead to unexpected behavior and security gaps.

After writing the ACL, the next step is to apply it to the appropriate interface and in the correct direction. ACLs can be applied inbound, meaning they filter traffic as it arrives at the interface, or outbound, meaning they filter traffic as it leaves the interface. The choice between inbound and outbound application depends on the desired control point. Inbound ACLs are typically used when blocking unwanted traffic as early as possible, conserving processing power and network resources. Outbound ACLs, on the other hand, are used when decisions need to be made after traffic has been processed internally. Applying the ACL in the wrong direction can render it ineffective or even disrupt legitimate operations.

Verifying and testing ACLs before deploying them in a production environment is a crucial part of the process. Because ACLs can impact connectivity and application performance, they should be tested in a controlled environment to ensure they behave as intended. Many devices offer simulation or preview tools that allow administrators to see how packets would be treated under a given ACL configuration. Monitoring tools and logs can also be used to confirm that the ACL is allowing or denying traffic as expected. This phase is especially important in complex networks where multiple ACLs may be interacting and where unintended consequences can result in outages or security breaches.

Documentation and maintenance are often overlooked but vital aspects of managing ACLs. Over time, networks evolve, new devices are added, services change, and business requirements shift. Without clear documentation, it becomes difficult to understand why a particular rule was created or whether it is still necessary. Proper naming conventions, comments within the ACL configuration, and regular audits help keep ACLs manageable and relevant. Stale or redundant rules not only clutter the configuration but also increase the risk of conflict and inefficiency. Maintaining ACLs as living documents ensures they continue to serve their intended purpose as the network grows and changes.

Creating and applying ACLs is not a one-time task but an ongoing responsibility. Network administrators must remain vigilant, continuously reviewing and updating access control rules to adapt to new threats and changing operational needs. The effectiveness of ACLs relies heavily on attention to detail, a deep understanding of the network environment, and a commitment to maintaining consistency and clarity in rule design. When thoughtfully created and properly applied, ACLs provide a powerful mechanism for enforcing security, ensuring compliance, and maintaining control over network resources. Their proper use can significantly reduce the attack surface, improve performance, and contribute to a robust and resilient network infrastructure.

ACL Wildcard Masking Techniques

ACL wildcard masking is a critical concept that network administrators must understand to configure effective and precise Access Control Lists. Unlike subnet masks, which define which portion of an IP address identifies the network and which portion identifies the host, wildcard masks are used in ACLs to determine which bits of an IP address should be examined and which should be ignored when applying filtering rules. Wildcard masks provide a flexible and powerful way to match single IP addresses, entire subnets, ranges of addresses, or even specific address patterns with a high level of control. Mastering wildcard masking techniques is essential for writing ACL entries that are both accurate and efficient, reducing unnecessary complexity while enforcing strict security policies.

The basic principle behind a wildcard mask is that it uses binary values to tell the router or firewall how to interpret each bit of an IP address. A binary zero in the wildcard mask means that the corresponding bit in the IP address must match exactly. A binary one means that the bit can be anything, essentially acting as a wildcard. This is the opposite of how a subnet mask works, which uses ones to identify the network portion and zeros for the host portion. For example, a wildcard mask of 0.0.0.0 applied to an IP address means that all bits must match exactly, which effectively targets a single host. On the other hand, a wildcard mask of 0.0.0.255 allows the last octet to vary, matching all addresses in that range.

Understanding how to calculate and apply wildcard masks correctly is vital. A common approach is to subtract each octet of a subnet mask from 255 to obtain the corresponding wildcard mask. For instance, a subnet mask of 255.255.255.0 would convert to a wildcard mask of 0.0.0.255. This conversion helps define ACL rules that match entire subnets. If an administrator wants to permit or deny access to all hosts within a specific subnet, such as 192.168.10.0/24, using the IP address 192.168.10.0 and wildcard mask 0.0.0.255 will match all addresses from 192.168.10.0 through 192.168.10.255.

In more complex scenarios, wildcard masks can be used to match specific patterns or ranges of IP addresses that do not align neatly with subnet boundaries. For example, an administrator may wish to match only even-numbered hosts or a custom block of addresses that falls within a larger subnet. This can be accomplished by carefully crafting a wildcard mask that accounts for binary variations in specific bits. Such precision requires a solid understanding of binary arithmetic, as each bit in the wildcard mask corresponds to a level of variation in the matched address. A wildcard mask of 0.0.0.3, for example, matches a range of four IP addresses because the last two bits in the final octet are set to one, allowing for variations in those positions.

One of the powerful aspects of wildcard masking is its ability to include or exclude specific portions of the address space with minimal rules. Instead of writing multiple ACL entries for several individual hosts or small subnets, a well-designed wildcard mask can encompass all of them with a single rule. This not only simplifies the configuration but also improves performance, as fewer rules mean less processing overhead for the device handling the ACL. Efficient wildcard usage is especially valuable in large networks where ACLs must manage thousands of hosts and services with minimal impact on traffic flow.

Wildcard masking is also helpful when applying ACLs for Quality of Service (QoS), routing control, and policy-based routing. By matching traffic from specific groups of IP addresses, administrators can apply differentiated treatment based on user role, department, or location. For example, an ACL using a wildcard mask can match all traffic from a group of branch offices and apply QoS policies to ensure their voice traffic receives priority over regular data. Similarly, in route filtering, wildcard masks help define which routing updates are accepted or advertised, allowing for better control over routing table contents and network stability.

Despite its power, wildcard masking is often a source of misconfiguration. One common mistake is reversing the logic and applying subnet mask thinking to wildcard masks, leading to incorrect address matches and unintentional permission or denial of traffic. Another frequent issue is using overly broad wildcard masks that unintentionally permit traffic from untrusted sources. For example, using 0.0.255.255 as a wildcard mask on a Class B address will match far more hosts than intended if the administrator is not careful. To avoid these pitfalls, it is essential to test ACLs in a lab environment, use packet tracing tools, and verify results with logging to ensure the rules perform as expected.

Named ACLs and modern network management platforms make working with wildcard masks easier by providing context and documentation capabilities. Including comments in ACL configurations can clarify the purpose of specific wildcard masks, aiding future maintenance and troubleshooting. In large organizations where multiple teams manage network devices, this documentation becomes critical to avoiding configuration errors and ensuring that access control remains aligned with business and security policies.

Wildcard masking techniques are also vital in dynamic environments such as cloud and hybrid networks, where IP addressing schemes may change frequently. Automation tools that generate ACLs based on templates or policy definitions must incorporate accurate wildcard masks to ensure consistent security across diverse platforms. By integrating wildcard logic into automated workflows, administrators can reduce human error, respond more quickly to network changes, and maintain a high level of security compliance across distributed infrastructures.

ACL wildcard masks continue to play a crucial role even in networks that use more advanced technologies such as context-based access control or next-generation firewalls. While these systems may offer more intuitive graphical interfaces and identity-based policies, the underlying packet filtering logic often still relies on the same principles of wildcard matching. For administrators working at the command-line level or in constrained environments, the ability to write precise and effective ACLs using wildcard masks remains a key competency.

Mastering wildcard masking techniques allows network professionals to take full advantage of ACLs as powerful tools for traffic control and security enforcement. Through careful planning, attention to binary detail, and thoughtful application of these masks, administrators can design efficient, scalable, and secure network policies. Wildcard masks are not merely technical details; they are strategic components that, when used skillfully, can transform basic access rules into finely tuned instruments of network governance.

Troubleshooting ACL Issues

Troubleshooting Access Control List (ACL) issues is a fundamental skill for any network administrator, as misconfigured or improperly applied ACLs can disrupt communication, block legitimate traffic, and create security vulnerabilities. ACLs are powerful tools designed to permit or deny traffic based on a wide range of conditions, but their strength also lies in their complexity. Even a small error in syntax, rule ordering, or wildcard masking can have widespread and unintended consequences across a network. Diagnosing and resolving ACL-related problems requires a structured approach, deep familiarity with how ACLs function, and the ability to interpret how the network behaves in real-time.

The first step in troubleshooting any ACL issue is identifying whether the ACL is actually the cause of the problem. Symptoms of ACL-related errors often include users being unable to reach specific servers, services appearing intermittently accessible, or routing behaviors not performing as expected. In such cases, it is important to gather basic information from users and network logs to understand the scope of the issue. Determining what is being blocked, from where, and under what conditions provides a starting point for analysis. A clear understanding of the problem will help differentiate between ACL issues and other potential causes like DNS errors, routing loops, or hardware failures.

One of the most common mistakes that leads to ACL problems is incorrect rule order. ACLs process entries from top to bottom and apply the first rule that matches a given packet. Once a match is found, no further rules are evaluated. If a broad deny rule is placed before a more specific permit rule, traffic that should be allowed may be dropped prematurely. For example, denying an entire subnet before allowing access to a single host within that subnet will result in the host being denied as well. Troubleshooting this requires reviewing the ACL line by line, checking for logic errors, and ensuring that specific exceptions are placed before general rules. Using sequence numbers in named ACLs can make it easier to adjust the order without rewriting the entire list.

Another frequent issue arises from incorrect wildcard masks. These masks are often confused with subnet masks, but their logic is fundamentally different. A wildcard mask defines which bits of an IP address should be ignored and which should be matched. Miscalculating a wildcard mask can result in rules that apply to unintended ranges of IP addresses. For instance, intending to permit traffic from a small subnet but writing a mask that covers a much broader range could inadvertently open access to untrusted devices. Conversely, writing a mask that is too narrow could block legitimate hosts. To troubleshoot wildcard mask problems, convert the mask to binary and compare it to the intended IP range, ensuring the logic aligns with the desired outcome.

Directionality is another common pitfall. ACLs can be applied in the inbound or outbound direction on an interface, and applying a rule in the wrong direction means it will never be triggered, leading to confusion during diagnostics. For example, applying an inbound ACL on an interface expecting to control outbound traffic will have no effect on the actual data flow. Diagnosing this issue requires verifying the flow of traffic and confirming the ACL is applied on the correct interface and in the correct direction relative to that flow. Using commands to inspect interface configurations and verify ACL bindings is essential during this phase.

Implicit deny is a built-in behavior of ACLs that often leads to unintended access problems. If a packet does not match any of the listed rules in an ACL, it is implicitly denied. This rule is not written explicitly in most configurations, so it can be overlooked when trying to understand why certain traffic is being dropped. To address this, administrators often add a final logging rule to catch unmatched traffic. For example, adding a deny any log statement at the end of the ACL can generate logs for all packets that are not explicitly permitted. These logs can provide valuable insight into what traffic is being dropped and why.

Syntax errors and misapplied commands are also frequent culprits. A small typographical mistake in an IP address, protocol type, or port number can invalidate a rule or cause it to match the wrong traffic. Even missing a keyword like eq or using tcp instead of udp can drastically alter the behavior of the ACL. To troubleshoot syntax issues, administrators should carefully compare the current ACL configuration to documented policies, looking for inconsistencies or anomalies. Many network devices offer commands to preview ACL configurations, validate syntax, or display compiled rules, all of which help in identifying mistakes before they impact the network.

Testing and simulation are valuable tools during the troubleshooting process. Packet tracer utilities and simulation environments allow administrators to test ACLs without affecting production traffic. These tools can show how a specific packet would be processed by an ACL, helping confirm whether the current rules produce the desired outcome. Additionally, capturing live traffic using tools like Wireshark can provide insight into what packets are hitting the ACL and whether they are being permitted or denied as intended. Combining these tools with logs generated by the firewall or router gives a comprehensive view of how traffic is being treated.

Collaborating with other teams and maintaining thorough documentation can significantly reduce the time required to troubleshoot ACL issues. Often, ACLs are created and managed by different teams over time, leading to rule sets that reflect outdated policies or temporary fixes that were never removed. Keeping a detailed record of who created each rule, why it was created, and when it was last reviewed helps prevent confusion and provides a reference during troubleshooting. When ACLs are treated as static and left unchecked, they accumulate obsolete entries that can conflict with new requirements or create blind spots in security coverage.

As networks become more dynamic, with the adoption of virtualization, cloud services, and software-defined networking, ACL troubleshooting must evolve as well. Dynamic environments require ACLs that adapt in real time to changes in infrastructure. Tools that automate ACL creation based on templates or centralized policies can reduce human error, but they still require validation and ongoing monitoring. Even in these advanced scenarios, the same principles apply: validate rule logic, verify application direction, check wildcard masks, and observe traffic behavior. The ability to interpret logs, correlate traffic patterns, and adjust configurations remains as important as ever.

Troubleshooting ACL issues demands both technical precision and a systematic approach. It combines detailed knowledge of networking fundamentals with practical experience in managing real-world configurations. While ACLs are one of the oldest and most established tools in network security, their continued relevance depends on the administrator's ability to configure them correctly and respond quickly when things go wrong. A well-trained eye, supported by good documentation and the right diagnostic tools, is often all it takes to resolve even the most perplexing ACL issues and restore proper functionality to the network.

Named ACLs for Improved Management

As networks expand and become more complex, the need for scalable, clear, and manageable configurations becomes increasingly important. In the context of Access Control Lists, named ACLs offer a more organized and flexible approach compared to their traditional numbered counterparts. Named ACLs enhance readability, simplify rule management, and support additional features that improve long-term administration. While both standard and extended ACLs can be implemented using numeric identifiers, named ACLs allow administrators to assign meaningful names to access control policies, making it easier to understand their purpose and maintain them over time.

Traditional numbered ACLs are identified by specific numeric ranges, such as 1 to 99 for standard ACLs and 100 to 199 for extended ACLs. These numbers are rigid, and while effective for small-scale networks or simple filtering tasks, they lack the descriptive power needed in larger environments. As more ACLs are created across a network, remembering what each number represents becomes increasingly difficult. Without comments or documentation, understanding the purpose behind each rule set requires digging into the configuration itself, line by line. This becomes especially problematic in environments with multiple administrators or when reviewing configurations after months or years of deployment.

Named ACLs address this issue by allowing administrators to define ACLs with textual identifiers. Instead of associating a rule set with an arbitrary number, a name can be assigned that describes its function or the part of the network it governs. For example, an ACL named Block_Guest_to_Internal or Permit_Admin_HTTP immediately communicates its intent. This not only improves clarity but also reduces the risk of misconfigurations, especially when multiple ACLs are in use. New administrators can more quickly understand and adapt to the existing structure without requiring extensive documentation or reverse-engineering of numerical ACLs.

In addition to improved readability, named ACLs introduce greater flexibility in rule editing. Unlike numbered ACLs, which typically require rewriting the entire list when changes are needed, named ACLs support the insertion or removal of individual entries. This is done through the use of sequence numbers, which determine the order in which rules are processed. Each rule in a named ACL can be assigned a specific sequence number, allowing new rules to be inserted in the correct place without disrupting the entire list. This feature is particularly valuable in dynamic environments where access policies change frequently and administrators must make adjustments without introducing downtime or configuration errors.

Named ACLs also support in-place editing, meaning individual rules can be modified or deleted without removing the whole ACL. This reduces the time and effort required to maintain the ACL and minimizes the chance of errors when updating access policies. For example, if a particular IP address needs to be excluded from a previously permitted range, an administrator can simply insert a deny statement with a lower sequence number. The remaining rules remain intact and continue to function as designed. This granular control makes named ACLs more practical for enterprise-scale networks and aligns with modern configuration management practices.

Another advantage of named ACLs is their compatibility with modern network automation and policy-based management systems. Because named ACLs use identifiers that are easier to interpret, they integrate more smoothly into scripts, templates, and configuration tools. Network automation platforms can reference ACLs by name, ensuring consistent deployment across multiple devices without relying on hard-coded numeric ranges. This facilitates repeatability, reduces human error, and supports large-scale policy enforcement across diverse environments.

Named ACLs are also more conducive to collaborative environments. In large organizations, network configuration is often handled by teams rather than individuals. Clear naming conventions and structured rule sets improve communication between team members, reducing confusion and promoting a shared understanding of security and access policies. When changes are needed, having named ACLs in place allows teams to coordinate updates more efficiently, with each member able to quickly identify the correct ACL to modify and understand its intended purpose.

Documentation and auditing are further enhanced by using named ACLs. Because names can reflect their function, they are easier to track in change logs, compliance reports, and access audits. For regulatory frameworks that require clear access control documentation, such as PCI-DSS or HIPAA, named ACLs provide an added layer of traceability. Each ACL name can be linked to a business requirement or policy, ensuring that access rules are aligned with operational and legal obligations. When audit teams review access configurations, named ACLs help demonstrate that the organization has a structured and well-documented approach to traffic control.

In terms of security, the clarity provided by named ACLs can prevent misconfigurations that might otherwise expose the network to vulnerabilities. When administrators clearly understand the intent behind each ACL, they are less likely to create overlapping or conflicting rules that could inadvertently permit unauthorized access or block legitimate traffic. The ability to isolate specific access requirements and define them clearly through named ACLs supports the principle of least privilege, ensuring that only the necessary traffic is permitted and everything else is appropriately restricted.

When implementing named ACLs, adopting consistent naming conventions is essential. Names should be descriptive but concise, using prefixes or suffixes that categorize the ACL by function, scope, or associated department. This standardization helps maintain a coherent structure and makes it easier to search and identify ACLs across devices. For example, a naming convention might include the device role, traffic direction, and protocol being controlled, resulting in names like EDGE_INBOUND_SSH or CORE_OUTBOUND_WEB. By following a naming scheme, organizations can avoid duplication, ensure logical organization, and streamline future maintenance.

Named ACLs represent an evolution in how access control policies are created, maintained, and understood. While they offer the same basic capabilities as numbered ACLs in terms of traffic filtering, their advantages in manageability, clarity, and scalability make them the preferred choice in modern networks. As networks grow more dynamic and policies become more complex, the need for human-readable, flexible, and easily modifiable configurations becomes ever more important. Named ACLs meet this need by providing administrators with the tools to manage access control in a way that is intuitive, efficient, and resilient to the demands of evolving network infrastructure. Their role in supporting automation, collaboration, and compliance ensures that they will remain a best practice for years to come.

Time-Based ACLs

Time-based Access Control Lists extend the capabilities of traditional ACLs by adding the dimension of time to traffic filtering policies. This feature allows network administrators to create rules that are active only during specific periods, offering more granular control over when access is granted or denied. By incorporating time constraints into ACL logic, organizations can enhance security, optimize resource use, and enforce business policies more effectively. This type of ACL is particularly useful in environments where access needs vary depending on the time of day, day of the week, or particular dates, such as holidays or maintenance windows.

The foundation of time-based ACLs lies in the use of time ranges that define when specific permit or deny statements should be active. A time range is a configuration element that specifies start and end times, recurring periods, or absolute calendar dates. Once defined, these time ranges can be referenced within ACL rules to apply them only during the designated periods. This means a rule that permits traffic to a server or blocks access to a specific network can be dynamically activated or deactivated based on the current time. The system clock on the network device is used to determine whether the current time falls within the specified range, which directly influences whether the ACL rule is applied.

One of the most common use cases for time-based ACLs is to restrict internet access in office environments during non-working hours. For example, a company may wish to allow employees to browse the web only during lunch breaks or after hours to ensure productivity during core business periods. By using a time-based ACL, the network administrator can create a rule that permits outbound HTTP and HTTPS traffic only between noon and 1 p.m., and again after 5 p.m. When the clock moves outside of these windows, the permit rule is no longer active, and a default deny rule can take effect, automatically blocking internet access without requiring manual intervention.

Another valuable application is securing access to critical infrastructure during limited time frames. For instance, system administrators may need to access sensitive servers for updates or maintenance, but only during designated change windows. A time-based ACL can be configured to allow SSH or RDP traffic only on Saturdays from 2 a.m. to 6 a.m., thereby reducing the attack surface during other times when access should not occur. This also adds an extra layer of control on top of traditional authentication methods, reinforcing the principle of least privilege by ensuring that access is not only role-based but also time-bound.

Time-based ACLs are particularly effective in educational institutions where access to specific online content must be controlled. Schools may choose to block social media or streaming services during classroom hours to keep students focused but allow access during lunch or after-school periods. In such cases, time-based ACLs help enforce acceptable use policies without requiring manual configuration changes throughout the day. The automation of rule enforcement based on time reduces the administrative burden while ensuring consistent policy adherence.

Implementing time-based ACLs requires careful planning and accurate configuration. The time range must be defined using precise syntax, specifying start and end times along with optional recurrence patterns. Depending on the device and operating system, the configuration can support absolute start and end times for one-time use or recurring rules based on weekdays, weekends, or specific calendar days. It is critical that the system clock is properly synchronized with an accurate time source, such as a Network Time Protocol (NTP) server. If the system clock is incorrect or drifts significantly, the time-based ACLs may activate or deactivate at unintended times, potentially causing service disruptions or security lapses.

Another aspect to consider when implementing time-based ACLs is the interaction between time-bound and static rules. A typical ACL may include both time-based and always-active rules, and the order of these entries affects how traffic is processed. Time-based entries must be carefully placed in the ACL to ensure they take precedence or defer to other rules as intended. Since ACLs process entries sequentially, a deny rule placed above a time-based permit rule could override it entirely, making it ineffective regardless of the time. Administrators must review rule order and logic to avoid conflicts and ensure that time-based controls function as expected.

Monitoring and troubleshooting time-based ACLs can be more challenging than with standard ACLs because the rule activation is conditional. When diagnosing access issues, administrators need to confirm whether a time-based rule is currently active and whether the correct time range is being enforced. Debugging tools and logs that show time-based rule evaluation are essential for verifying the correct operation of these ACLs. Some systems provide commands to display currently active rules and the status of associated time ranges, which can help in identifying misconfigurations or mismatches between expected and actual behavior.

From a security perspective, time-based ACLs add a dynamic layer of defense that can help reduce the risk of unauthorized access during vulnerable periods. By disabling access when it is not needed, organizations reduce the opportunity for attacks that rely on timing, such as exploiting unattended services during off-hours. This can be particularly valuable in protecting remote access services, where restricting login attempts to specific windows of time can significantly narrow the exposure to brute-force or credential-based attacks.

In environments where compliance and auditing are critical, time-based ACLs also help demonstrate control over access policies. Regulatory standards often require that access to certain systems be limited and that policies are enforced automatically. Time-based ACLs provide an auditable mechanism for such enforcement, allowing organizations to show that access is not only role-specific but also restricted to approved times. Logs of time-based rule activations and the associated access attempts can support compliance reports and incident investigations.

The use of time-based ACLs continues to grow as organizations seek to implement smarter, more responsive network policies. Whether managing bandwidth, enforcing productivity, protecting critical assets, or meeting compliance requirements, time-based ACLs offer a level of automation and precision that static rules cannot match. By combining temporal logic with traditional filtering criteria, network administrators can create policies that adapt to the rhythm of the business, enhancing both security and efficiency. This flexibility makes time-based ACLs a powerful tool in the modern network administrator's toolkit, capable of aligning access control with real-world schedules and operational realities.

Reflexive ACLs Explained

Reflexive Access Control Lists, also known as dynamic ACLs, provide a more intelligent and state-aware mechanism for filtering traffic in comparison to traditional static ACLs. Unlike standard and extended ACLs, which are unidirectional and rely solely on fixed rules, reflexive ACLs introduce the ability to monitor and respond to traffic flows dynamically. They do this by tracking active sessions initiated from within the trusted internal network and then creating temporary, automatically generated entries to allow corresponding return traffic. This approach offers a balance between security and functionality, making it a powerful option for environments that require control over outbound sessions and tight restrictions on unsolicited inbound traffic.

At the core of reflexive ACL functionality is the concept of session awareness. When a device within the internal network initiates a connection to an external destination, a reflexive ACL creates a temporary rule based on the characteristics of the outbound session. These characteristics include source and destination IP addresses, protocol type, and port numbers. This temporary rule permits the response traffic to return through the firewall or router, as long as it matches the parameters of the original session. Once the session is terminated or a predefined timeout is reached, the temporary rule is automatically deleted, closing the window for return traffic and restoring the ACL to its default restrictive state.

This dynamic behavior addresses a critical limitation of traditional ACLs: the inability to differentiate between legitimate return traffic and unsolicited inbound traffic. Static ACLs must explicitly define both inbound and outbound rules, making it difficult to maintain security without inadvertently blocking valid communication or opening unnecessary access. Reflexive ACLs solve this problem by allowing only return traffic that is directly associated with sessions initiated from within the trusted network. This means that unsolicited attempts to establish connections from the outside are automatically denied, unless specific rules are configured to allow them.

To implement reflexive ACLs, administrators must define extended named ACLs and include special keywords that instruct the router or firewall to monitor outbound sessions and generate corresponding inbound rules. Typically, the outbound ACL includes a statement that reflects traffic, meaning it creates the temporary rule for the return path. The inbound ACL then evaluates return traffic against the temporary entries to determine whether to permit or deny it. This two-part configuration requires careful coordination to ensure that the reflected rules match only valid sessions and that they are placed on the correct interfaces and directions within the network topology.

One of the key benefits of reflexive ACLs is the increased security they provide without significantly compromising usability. In a traditional ACL setup, administrators often struggle to create rules that permit return traffic while blocking unauthorized access. This can lead to overly permissive rules that expose the network to risks. Reflexive ACLs eliminate this tradeoff by allowing return traffic only when it is associated with a known, active outbound session. This tight coupling between outgoing and incoming traffic minimizes the exposure to potential threats such as unsolicited scans, spoofed packets, and brute-force attacks.

Reflexive ACLs are particularly useful in environments that do not use full stateful inspection firewalls but still require dynamic control over connections. While stateful firewalls provide similar functionality with more sophisticated session tracking, they are not always available or feasible in all network segments, especially in routers with basic filtering capabilities. Reflexive ACLs bring some of the advantages of stateful inspection to environments that rely on ACL-based security, offering a bridge between static filtering and more advanced security architectures.

However, deploying reflexive ACLs comes with certain challenges and limitations. One of the primary concerns is the increase in configuration complexity. Because reflexive ACLs involve dynamic entries and interaction between inbound and outbound rules, administrators must carefully design their configurations to ensure consistency and predictability. Misconfigured rules or misplaced ACLs can lead to traffic being unintentionally blocked or permitted. Troubleshooting these issues requires a solid understanding of how reflexive ACLs function and how session information is tracked and aged.

Performance is another factor to consider. Since reflexive ACLs create and maintain temporary entries for each active session, they can consume additional memory and processing resources on the network device. In high-traffic environments with many concurrent sessions, this can lead to resource exhaustion or reduced performance. Network administrators must monitor device utilization and be cautious about using reflexive ACLs in situations where the device may not have sufficient capacity to handle the dynamic overhead.

Another limitation is that reflexive ACLs are not as flexible as stateful inspection when it comes to handling complex protocols or applications that use multiple ports or dynamically negotiated connections. For example, some multimedia applications or certain types of FTP sessions may not function correctly through a reflexive ACL because the return traffic may not match the exact parameters of the original session, especially if additional ports are involved. In such cases, exceptions may need to be made, or additional protocols handled through more advanced security solutions.

Logging and visibility are also important when working with reflexive ACLs. Since the rules are dynamic and temporary, administrators must use diagnostic commands and logging features to observe how traffic is being matched and filtered in real time. Many routers and firewalls provide tools to display the active reflexive entries and their associated session details. These tools are essential for verifying that the configuration is working as intended and for diagnosing issues with traffic flow. Without proper monitoring, it can be difficult to understand whether traffic is being dropped due to ACL rules or other network issues.

Despite these challenges, reflexive ACLs remain a valuable tool in the network security toolbox. They provide a level of intelligent traffic control that bridges the gap between static filtering and full stateful inspection. When used appropriately, they enhance security by reducing the attack surface and preventing unauthorized inbound traffic, while still allowing necessary outbound communication. Their dynamic nature aligns well with modern network demands, where flexibility and responsiveness are critical to maintaining secure and efficient operations.

To maximize the benefits of reflexive ACLs, network administrators should follow best practices such as defining clear session timeouts, regularly reviewing active sessions, and maintaining synchronized configurations across devices. Documentation is essential to ensure that the logic behind the ACL rules is understood by all team members and can be updated as the network evolves. Reflexive ACLs offer a blend of automation and control that, when properly implemented, can significantly strengthen a network's defense against external threats without sacrificing functionality or performance.

Dynamic ACLs and Authentication

Dynamic Access Control Lists introduce a level of interactivity and flexibility to traditional ACL configurations by integrating user authentication into the process of access control. Unlike static ACLs, which are permanently configured and enforced regardless of user identity or session status, dynamic ACLs are created and applied in real time, typically in response to a successful authentication event. This model allows network administrators to implement security policies that adapt to the specific user or device attempting to access the network, enabling more granular and context-aware traffic filtering. By combining access control with authentication mechanisms, dynamic ACLs support stronger security practices and provide better alignment with organizational policies regarding user roles and privileges.

At the core of dynamic ACLs is the concept of conditional access. Access is not granted simply because a packet matches an IP address or port number; instead, access is dynamically permitted based on the outcome of an authentication process. When a user attempts to connect to a network resource, they are redirected to an authentication server, typically using protocols such as RADIUS or TACACS+. Once the user provides valid credentials and their identity is verified, the authentication server communicates with the network device, instructing it to temporarily permit access by installing a user-specific ACL. This ACL remains in place only for the duration of the authenticated session and is removed automatically when the session ends or after a timeout occurs.

This method of access control provides several advantages. First, it enhances security by ensuring that only authenticated users can reach protected resources. Unlike static ACLs that rely on IP addresses—which can be spoofed or shared—dynamic ACLs tie access directly to the identity of the user. This significantly reduces the chances of unauthorized access and supports the enforcement of user-specific policies. For example, an administrator might be allowed access to internal management interfaces, while a regular user is restricted to general services such as email and web browsing. These differentiated access levels are enforced dynamically based on who the user is and what role they hold within the organization.

Another key benefit of dynamic ACLs is their support for temporary access scenarios. In many organizations, there are legitimate cases where users need short-term access to specific systems or services. These might include contractors, consultants, or employees performing special tasks outside their normal responsibilities. Instead of permanently modifying firewall rules or maintaining large static ACLs that account for every possible exception, administrators can use dynamic ACLs to grant time-limited access based on authentication. When the task is complete or the session ends, the access is revoked automatically, minimizing risk and administrative overhead.

Implementing dynamic ACLs typically requires integration with a centralized authentication system and a network device capable of interpreting and applying dynamic policies. The process begins with a user connecting to the network and triggering an authentication request. This might occur through a login prompt at a terminal server, a VPN gateway, or a network access control system such as 802.1X. The authentication server validates the user's credentials and sends a response that includes the access permissions to be applied. These permissions are translated into an ACL that the network device enforces for the session. This process can be tailored to include additional conditions, such as device posture, time of day, or network location, further refining the access control decision.

One common use case of dynamic ACLs is in controlling access to campus or enterprise networks where users bring their own devices. Rather than assigning full access to anyone who connects, the network uses authentication to determine the user's role and applies a corresponding access policy. Students may be allowed internet access only, faculty may have access to internal academic resources, and IT staff may be granted access to administrative systems. The ACLs enforcing these policies are created dynamically and reflect the specific needs and permissions of each group. This approach is far more scalable and secure than attempting to manage a comprehensive set of static rules for every user type.

Despite their benefits, dynamic ACLs also introduce certain complexities. Because they depend on successful authentication and coordination between multiple systems, there are more points of potential failure. A misconfigured authentication server, communication error between devices, or timeout inconsistency can result in users being denied access or granted unintended permissions. Troubleshooting these issues requires visibility into both the authentication process and the dynamic policy application. Logs, debug tools, and monitoring systems become essential components in maintaining a healthy dynamic ACL deployment.

Another consideration is the performance impact of managing many dynamic entries. Each user or session requires the generation and maintenance of specific rules, which can consume memory and CPU resources on the network device. In high-volume environments with thousands of concurrent users, this may necessitate capacity planning and hardware considerations. Network devices must be selected and configured to support the dynamic ACL features effectively without degrading performance under load.

Policy management also becomes more critical when using dynamic ACLs. Because access decisions are made dynamically, based on attributes provided by the authentication server, it is important to have clear and consistent definitions of user roles, permissions, and conditions. These definitions must be maintained in a central policy repository and kept up to date as organizational needs evolve. Regular reviews and audits help ensure that policies remain aligned with business objectives and compliance requirements.

Dynamic ACLs also provide opportunities for integration with broader identity and access management systems. By linking network access policies with centralized identity repositories such as Active Directory or LDAP, organizations can achieve consistent enforcement of access controls across both network and application layers. This integration supports a more holistic security posture, where user identity becomes the central factor in determining what resources can be accessed, from where, and under what conditions. As organizations adopt zero trust models, dynamic ACLs fit naturally into architectures that require continuous validation of user identity and context.

In a world where networks are increasingly mobile, cloud-connected, and user-centric, static methods of access control are no longer sufficient to meet the demands of security and flexibility. Dynamic ACLs represent a significant advancement by allowing the network to respond in real time to changes in user identity and access requirements. Their integration with authentication systems provides a powerful mechanism for enforcing security policies that are both adaptive and enforceable at the network perimeter. By leveraging dynamic ACLs, organizations can reduce risk, improve efficiency, and maintain tighter control over who can access what, when, and how— without sacrificing usability or scalability.

Best Practices for ACL Deployment

Deploying Access Control Lists effectively requires more than just writing permit and deny statements. ACLs play a critical role in enforcing security policies, shaping traffic, and protecting network resources from unauthorized access. However, when implemented poorly, they can introduce misconfigurations that result in service disruptions, security vulnerabilities, or unintentional access. To ensure that ACLs serve their intended purpose while maintaining network stability and security, administrators must follow a set of best practices that address the technical, operational, and strategic aspects of ACL design and deployment. These practices are not simply recommendations—they are foundational principles that, when followed consistently, support scalable and secure network architectures.

One of the first best practices in ACL deployment is the principle of least privilege. Every ACL should be designed to grant the minimum necessary permissions required for a specific task or function. Rather than allowing broad access, ACLs should explicitly define which users, systems, or networks are allowed to communicate, and only through the specific ports and protocols needed for their operation. This approach minimizes the attack surface and reduces the likelihood of unauthorized access, whether accidental or malicious. Overly permissive ACLs often lead to security incidents because they expose resources unnecessarily or allow unintended services to pass through the network perimeter.

Clarity in rule definitions is equally important. Each entry in an ACL should be precise and easily understandable, both in its function and scope. Avoiding vague or ambiguous rules improves not only the immediate effectiveness of the ACL but also long-term manageability. For example, rather than writing a rule that permits all traffic from an entire subnet, administrators should restrict access to known IP addresses or ranges with a defined purpose. This specificity makes it easier to audit the ACL later, ensures better compliance with organizational policies, and prevents unanticipated interactions between rules.

Another best practice is to organize ACLs logically and consistently. This includes grouping similar rules together and using a standardized naming convention for ACL identifiers. Named ACLs are preferable over numbered ones because they provide greater context and are easier to track. Rules within an ACL should be ordered from most specific to most general. Because ACLs are processed sequentially from top to bottom, placing broader rules at the top may cause specific rules to be ignored. For example, a general deny rule should never precede a more specific permit rule unless the goal is to explicitly override exceptions. Understanding the processing logic of ACLs is key to creating an order of operations that reflects the intended access policies.

Regular documentation is essential for successful ACL deployment. Every ACL should be accompanied by notes or comments that explain the purpose of each rule, the systems it affects, and the justification for its existence. Documentation becomes especially valuable when multiple administrators manage network devices or when ACLs need to be audited for compliance purposes. It also helps when troubleshooting access issues, as administrators can quickly determine whether a particular rule is intentional or a misconfiguration. Properly documented ACLs also speed up onboarding for new team members and reduce dependency on institutional memory.

Testing is another critical component of ACL best practices. Before deploying any new ACL or modifying an existing one, administrators should test the configuration in a controlled environment to verify that it behaves as expected. Simulating traffic flows and validating the results with tools like packet tracers or network analyzers can uncover errors that might otherwise go unnoticed until they impact production systems. It is important to validate not only permitted traffic but also to confirm that unauthorized or unwanted traffic is successfully blocked. Testing should extend to verifying the impact of rule changes on dependent services, such as routing protocols, VPN tunnels, or management interfaces.

Monitoring and logging should be enabled wherever possible to track the effectiveness of ACLs in real time. Devices should log matches for specific rules, especially deny statements, so administrators can see what traffic is being dropped and why. These logs help identify misconfigurations, such as mistakenly blocked traffic, and can also alert administrators to potential security threats, such as repeated access attempts from suspicious IP addresses. When used effectively, logging provides critical insight into network behavior and supports faster troubleshooting and incident response.

ACLs should also be reviewed and updated regularly. As networks evolve, with new systems coming online and old ones being decommissioned, the relevance of existing ACL rules can change. Stale entries can clutter the configuration and create unnecessary processing overhead. Worse, they can provide access to resources that no longer need to be exposed. A periodic ACL review process ensures that rules remain aligned with current business requirements and security standards. This review should include not only technical validation but also stakeholder input to ensure that access decisions continue to reflect organizational priorities.

Maintaining consistency across network devices is vital for maintaining a secure and manageable environment. ACLs should be standardized wherever possible to enforce uniform policies across routers, firewalls, and switches. This can be achieved through the use of templates, configuration management tools, or centralized policy enforcement platforms. When different devices use different ACLs to enforce similar policies, the chances of conflict, redundancy, or gaps in coverage increase significantly. Uniform deployment supports auditability, simplifies troubleshooting, and reduces the risk of inconsistent behavior across different parts of the network.

One often overlooked best practice is planning for scalability from the start. ACL configurations that work well for small environments may not scale to meet the needs of growing networks. Writing ACLs with growth in mind means designing rules that are modular, easy to extend, and capable of handling new address ranges or services without major restructuring. Modular ACLs can be reused across devices or grouped into policy objects that simplify management. When combined with dynamic or context-based features, scalable ACLs support agility and responsiveness in changing network conditions.

Finally, integration with broader security policies and frameworks should always be considered. ACLs are just one part of a layered defense strategy that includes firewalls, intrusion detection systems, endpoint protection, and more. Their deployment should complement and reinforce the overall security architecture. This means aligning ACL policies with regulatory compliance requirements, data classification standards, and incident response plans. By integrating ACLs into the larger security posture, organizations can achieve more comprehensive protection and better resilience against evolving threats.

Deploying ACLs is not a one-time configuration task but an ongoing process of design, validation, maintenance, and improvement. Following best practices ensures that ACLs fulfill their role as gatekeepers of network traffic without becoming sources of disruption or risk. Through careful planning, disciplined implementation, and continuous refinement, ACLs remain one of the most powerful tools available for securing and managing modern network environments.

ACLs vs Firewall Rulesets

Access Control Lists and firewall rulesets are both essential components in the realm of network security, often used to regulate the flow of traffic and enforce access policies across network boundaries. While they serve similar purposes in controlling traffic, there are important differences between the two in terms of architecture, functionality, flexibility, and context. Understanding these distinctions is crucial for network administrators and security professionals who must decide when to use one over the other or how to integrate both effectively in a layered security model. Although ACLs and firewall rulesets may overlap in some capabilities, they are not interchangeable tools. Each has its own design philosophy, operational use cases, and deployment scenarios.

Access Control Lists are traditionally associated with routers and switches, primarily operating at Layers 3 and 4 of the OSI model. Their main role is to permit or deny packets based on criteria such as source and destination IP addresses, protocol types, and port numbers. ACLs are configured directly on network devices and are processed in a sequential, top-down order. Once a match is found in an ACL, the corresponding action is taken, and the rest of the list is not evaluated. This linear evaluation model is straightforward and efficient, making ACLs an ideal solution for basic packet filtering, traffic segmentation, and routing control. However, this simplicity also limits their depth of inspection and ability to respond to more sophisticated attack patterns.

Firewall rulesets, on the other hand, are typically implemented on dedicated security appliances or software platforms designed specifically to protect network perimeters and internal zones. Modern firewalls, especially next-generation firewalls, operate beyond the capabilities of traditional ACLs by providing deep packet inspection, application-level filtering, user identity awareness, and threat prevention features. They can examine traffic at multiple OSI layers, including Layer 7, allowing for a more nuanced and context-aware evaluation of traffic. This enables firewall rulesets to detect anomalies, enforce application-specific policies, and prevent known attacks using integrated intrusion prevention systems and threat intelligence feeds.

One of the key differences between ACLs and firewall rulesets is the scope of context available during rule evaluation. ACLs are stateless by default, meaning they evaluate each packet independently without regard for session state or traffic patterns. While there are extensions such as reflexive and dynamic ACLs that introduce limited statefulness, these implementations are not as robust as the full stateful inspection performed by firewalls. A firewall, by contrast, keeps track of active connections and uses this information to make informed decisions about whether packets are part of an established session or potentially malicious traffic. This stateful behavior allows firewalls to distinguish between legitimate and unsolicited traffic more effectively.

Another distinction lies in the granularity of control. ACLs provide basic control mechanisms, which are often sufficient for simple network segmentation or allowing specific services through certain interfaces. However, they lack the flexibility to enforce policies based on factors such as user identity, time of day, or device type. Firewall rulesets, especially in next-generation platforms, can include conditions based on authentication, geolocation, risk profiles, and behavioral analysis. This level of granularity supports complex enterprise security policies that require more than just IP-based filtering.

Management and scalability also differentiate ACLs from firewall rulesets. ACLs can become difficult to manage as they grow in size and complexity. Because they are typically configured manually using command-line interfaces, large ACLs can be cumbersome to update, audit, and troubleshoot. Mistakes in rule order or wildcard mask calculations can easily lead to security gaps or service disruptions. Firewall rule management, particularly in enterprise-grade solutions, often benefits from centralized graphical interfaces, rule logging, change tracking, and policy validation features. These management tools allow administrators to visualize rule impacts, simulate policy changes, and ensure compliance with internal standards or external regulations.

Logging and monitoring are more robust and comprehensive in firewalls compared to ACLs. Most ACL implementations offer only basic logging capabilities, often limited to indicating whether traffic matched a specific rule. In contrast, firewalls can generate detailed logs for every session, including timestamps, rule matches, applications detected, user identities, and actions taken. These logs are invaluable for security operations centers, providing data for forensic analysis, threat detection, and incident response. The integration of firewalls with security information and event management systems further enhances visibility across the network.

Deployment location also influences the choice between ACLs and firewall rulesets. ACLs are often deployed on internal routers or distribution layer switches to control inter-VLAN communication or apply simple access restrictions. Their low processing overhead makes them suitable for high-speed packet filtering in environments where complex analysis is not required. Firewalls, on the other hand, are positioned at network edges, between trust zones, or at critical access points where deeper inspection and policy enforcement are needed. Some organizations even deploy firewalls within internal segments to protect sensitive systems, using ACLs in conjunction with them for additional segmentation.

While ACLs can offer basic traffic control and remain a valuable part of network architecture, relying solely on them for security is insufficient in today's threat landscape. Modern attacks often leverage encrypted traffic, application vulnerabilities, or user-based exploits that are invisible to basic packet filters. Firewalls are equipped to handle these advanced threats, using signature-based detection, sandboxing, SSL decryption, and heuristic analysis to block malicious activity that ACLs cannot detect. This makes firewalls an essential component of any defense-in-depth strategy.

Despite their limitations, ACLs continue to play an important role when used appropriately. They can offload basic filtering tasks from firewalls, reduce unnecessary traffic before it reaches inspection points, and enforce simple but effective segmentation policies. For example, an ACL might be used to block traffic between departments that have no need to communicate, while the firewall focuses on inspecting external traffic and enforcing compliance requirements. In this way, ACLs and firewall rulesets complement each other, each handling aspects of traffic control suited to their strengths.

In hybrid environments where cloud, on-premises, and remote access converge, both ACLs and firewall rulesets must be adapted to support modern architectures. Cloud-native firewalls, virtual firewalls, and security groups function similarly to traditional firewalls but are designed to integrate with dynamic workloads and orchestrated environments. Likewise, ACLs can be applied in cloud networking platforms like AWS and Azure to restrict access to instances or services at the network interface level. The principles remain the same, but the implementation shifts to suit the infrastructure model.

Choosing between ACLs and firewall rulesets is not always a matter of one or the other. In many well-architected networks, both are used in tandem to achieve layered security. ACLs provide lightweight, fast filtering that reduces overhead on downstream systems, while firewalls deliver the depth and intelligence required to handle sophisticated threats. Understanding their respective strengths and limitations allows administrators to design networks that are secure, efficient, and capable of adapting to future demands. Integrating both technologies in a complementary fashion is key to building a resilient network defense posture that addresses the wide array of challenges faced in today's digital environments.

Introduction to Security Zones

Security zones are a foundational concept in network security architecture, serving as a method for logically segmenting a network into areas of varying trust levels and applying policies to control the flow of traffic between them. By grouping interfaces, devices, or entire subnets into clearly defined zones, administrators can better enforce access control, monitor communication patterns, and isolate sensitive resources from broader network exposure. The use of security zones introduces structure and clarity into what can otherwise be a flat, borderless network, where indiscriminate communication between systems increases the risk of unauthorized access, malware propagation, and data loss.

At its core, the purpose of security zoning is to compartmentalize the network based on security requirements. Each zone represents a collection of systems that share a similar trust level and function. A common implementation includes at least three core zones: an internal or trusted zone, an external or untrusted zone, and a demilitarized zone (DMZ) positioned between them. The internal zone typically contains enterprise workstations, internal servers, and other resources meant only for authorized personnel. The external zone represents the internet or other untrusted networks. The DMZ acts as a buffer, hosting systems that need to be accessible from the outside, such as web servers, mail servers, or VPN gateways, while still shielding the internal network from direct exposure.

This zone-based approach provides a logical framework for applying differentiated security policies. Communication within the same zone is typically unrestricted, assuming the systems within that zone are equally trusted. However, traffic that crosses from one zone to another is subject to inspection and filtering based on the organization's policies. For example, while internal clients may freely communicate with one another, a firewall may restrict or inspect all outbound communication from the internal zone to the internet. Similarly, traffic from the DMZ to the internal zone may be heavily restricted or even blocked entirely, depending on whether such communication is necessary.

One of the major benefits of using security zones is that they support the principle of least privilege. By segmenting the network into zones and tightly controlling what can pass between them, organizations limit the ability of users or systems to access resources they do not need. This not only helps reduce the risk of accidental exposure but also acts as a powerful mitigation strategy against breaches. If a threat actor compromises a device in one zone, the zone boundary becomes an obstacle that prevents or slows lateral movement across the network. This containment strategy is particularly effective against worms, ransomware, and advanced persistent threats, which rely on moving laterally to find high-value targets.

Creating effective security zones requires a deep understanding of the network's topology, business functions, and data flows. It is not enough to create arbitrary divisions; the segmentation must align with how the organization operates. Systems that serve similar roles or are used by the same departments may be grouped into the same zone, while high-value assets such as database servers, authentication services, or financial systems might be placed in more restricted zones with limited access. Modern enterprises may create zones based on a wide variety of criteria, including business units, regulatory compliance requirements, application types, or user roles.

Security zones also serve as a foundation for implementing zone-based firewalls. Unlike traditional interface-based firewalls that apply rules to specific interfaces, zone-based firewalls use the concept of zones to define policy. Each interface is assigned to a zone, and policies are created to define which types of traffic are allowed between zones. This approach not only simplifies policy management but also improves scalability and consistency across large networks. For example, a policy can be written to allow HTTP traffic from the user zone to the web zone, and that policy will apply to all interfaces associated with those zones, regardless of the physical topology.

In addition to simplifying policy enforcement, security zones improve visibility and auditing. When traffic is categorized by zone, administrators can more easily monitor and analyze flows between areas of different trust. This allows for better detection of anomalies, unauthorized access attempts, or misrouted data. Security zones also facilitate compliance with regulatory requirements that call for network segmentation, such as PCI-DSS, which mandates the isolation of cardholder data environments. By using zones to separate sensitive data from general-purpose systems, organizations can demonstrate a clear structure of control and limit the scope of compliance audits.

As network architectures evolve, especially with the rise of cloud computing, virtualization, and software-defined networking, the concept of security zones must evolve as well. In virtualized environments, zones may be defined logically using software policies rather than physical interfaces. Cloud providers offer constructs like security groups and virtual private clouds, which function similarly to traditional zones by isolating resources and controlling traffic. Hybrid architectures that span on-premises and cloud environments often require unified policy frameworks that maintain zone integrity across different platforms and technologies. Regardless of the implementation model, the underlying principles remain the same: isolate, control, monitor, and enforce.

Security zones are not limited to perimeter security. Internal segmentation, often referred to as microsegmentation, applies the zone concept within the internal network to further reduce risk. This can be particularly important in environments with a high density of virtual machines, user devices, or sensitive applications. By breaking down the internal network into smaller zones, organizations can achieve finer-grained control over internal traffic and better protect against insider threats or compromised systems. The granularity of microsegmentation extends the benefits of zoning deep into the core of the network, making it a powerful strategy for defense in depth.

Proper planning is essential when designing a zone-based architecture. Administrators must identify all critical assets, map their communication requirements, and determine the appropriate trust level for each system. Careful consideration must be given to how zones interact and where inspection or enforcement points are placed. Firewalls, intrusion prevention systems, and other controls must be strategically deployed to monitor and regulate inter-zone communication. Policy design should be driven by business requirements and risk assessments, not by convenience or legacy configurations. Zones should also be documented thoroughly, with clear definitions and rationales for each boundary, to support maintenance, audits, and incident response.

Ultimately, the concept of security zones brings order and control to the complex and often chaotic world of network traffic. By organizing systems according to trust and function, and by controlling interactions between them, zones create a structured environment that supports both security and operational efficiency. Whether used to separate internal departments, isolate sensitive data, or protect public-facing services, zones provide a scalable and effective method for managing network risk. As networks continue to grow in size and complexity, the disciplined use of security zones will remain a central strategy for building resilient and secure infrastructures.

Zone-Based Firewall Design

Zone-based firewall design is a modern and highly structured approach to network security that builds upon the concept of security zones to enforce access control policies. Unlike traditional access control mechanisms that apply rules directly to interfaces or specific IP addresses, zone-based firewalls rely on grouping interfaces into logical zones and then defining security policies that govern the traffic allowed between these zones. This method allows for more intuitive policy management, better scalability, and a stronger alignment between security architecture and organizational needs. As networks grow in complexity and demand more flexible control models, zone-based firewall design offers a framework that adapts to diverse environments without sacrificing clarity or security.

In a zone-based firewall model, the network is segmented into multiple zones, each representing a different level of trust or function. These zones could include internal networks, external networks, data centers, management systems, and demilitarized zones (DMZs). Interfaces on the firewall are assigned to one or more of these zones, and traffic between zones is explicitly allowed or denied based on policy. Unlike legacy firewalls that rely on implicit trust or default pass-through behaviors, zone-based firewalls treat each zone interaction as a unique relationship that must be defined. This strict model ensures that no traffic is permitted between zones unless it has been specifically authorized.

One of the key strengths of zone-based firewall design is its alignment with the principle of least privilege. Each zone is treated as a self-contained environment with its own rules, and communication is only enabled when there is a clear business or operational need. This limits unnecessary exposure and prevents lateral movement by attackers. For example, an internal user network may have access to internet services but not to the management network or sensitive databases, even if they reside on the same physical infrastructure. By requiring administrators to define explicit inter-zone policies, zone-based firewalls minimize the chances of over-permissive rules and accidental trust relationships.

Policy creation in a zone-based firewall follows a logical, structured format. Instead of applying a rule directly to a source and destination IP, administrators define a policy between source and destination zones. Within this policy, they specify the protocols, ports, and other conditions under which traffic is allowed. This abstraction simplifies configuration because it decouples security rules from specific network topology details. As interfaces change, devices are added, or IP ranges are reallocated, the zone relationships remain intact, and policies continue to function without needing extensive reconfiguration. This separation of control logic from physical layout is one of the major advantages of zone-based design.

Another benefit is improved readability and maintainability. When firewall rules are organized by zone relationships, it becomes much easier to understand the intended security posture of the network. Rather than sifting through hundreds of interface-bound rules, administrators can quickly review the traffic allowed between, for example, the user zone and the DMZ, or the production zone and the backup network. This clarity supports better policy review, auditing, and troubleshooting. When an access issue arises, the zone-based model makes it easier to trace the decision-making process, isolate the relevant policy, and implement necessary changes with minimal risk to unrelated systems.

Zone-based firewalls also support more advanced traffic inspection and control features. Policies can include stateful inspection, deep packet inspection, intrusion prevention, and even application-level filtering. These features are particularly useful in modern environments where threats are more sophisticated and traditional port-based filtering is no longer sufficient. A policy between a user zone and the internet might include SSL decryption, URL filtering, and malware scanning, while traffic between internal application zones might be inspected for abnormal behavior or policy violations. By anchoring these inspections to zone relationships, administrators can apply consistent protections across multiple systems without redundancy or gaps.

Deploying a zone-based firewall requires careful planning and an accurate understanding of the network's function and layout. The first step is to define the zones themselves, based on trust levels, roles, and data classification. Each zone should have a clearly articulated purpose, such as hosting user devices, public-facing services, internal applications, or sensitive data. Once zones are defined, interfaces are assigned accordingly, and policies are created to govern inter-zone traffic. During this phase, it is important to involve stakeholders from security, operations, and business units to ensure that the policies reflect actual workflows and risk tolerances.

Testing and validation are critical components of zone-based firewall implementation. Because the model is strict by default, failing to define a necessary policy will result in dropped traffic. While this prevents unauthorized access, it can also disrupt legitimate business functions if not properly anticipated. Administrators should use test environments, policy simulations, and traffic logs to verify that policies behave as intended. Any denied traffic should be analyzed to determine whether it represents a security threat or a misconfiguration. Over time, adjustments can be made to refine the policy set and optimize performance.

In dynamic environments such as cloud infrastructure, virtualization platforms, and software-defined networks, the zone-based model remains relevant and adaptable. Virtual firewalls and security appliances in these environments often support zone-based policy frameworks, allowing consistent enforcement across hybrid architectures. Security zones in the cloud may correspond to different virtual networks, regions, or resource groups, but the fundamental principles remain the same. Defining trust boundaries, assigning resources to zones, and controlling inter-zone traffic continues to be an effective strategy for securing modern workloads.

Zone-based firewall design also supports broader security frameworks such as zero trust. In a zero trust architecture, every access request is treated as potentially hostile, and verification is required at each step. By using zone-based policies, organizations can enforce segmentation that aligns with zero trust principles. Microsegmentation within internal zones further refines control, allowing policies to be applied not just between user and server zones, but between individual application components. This level of granularity enhances the ability to contain breaches, monitor behaviors, and enforce strict security policies without overwhelming complexity.

Ultimately, zone-based firewall design provides a clear and manageable way to enforce security in complex networks. It brings structure to policy creation, ensures consistent enforcement, and supports scalability as the network evolves. By grouping systems according to trust and function, and by requiring explicit policies for inter-zone communication, administrators gain precise control over how data flows through the network. This not only strengthens security but also simplifies ongoing management, enabling organizations to adapt more easily to changing threats, technologies, and business requirements. The zone-based approach continues to be a cornerstone of modern firewall architecture, offering a practical and effective solution for securing networks in an increasingly interconnected world.

Benefits of Zone Segmentation

Zone segmentation is a fundamental strategy in network security that enhances the overall protection, performance, and manageability of an IT environment. By dividing a network into multiple security zones based on trust levels, function, or sensitivity, organizations can gain more precise control over how traffic flows and which resources are accessible to whom. This segmentation not only enforces tighter security policies but also helps in isolating threats, minimizing the attack surface, and ensuring regulatory compliance. In an era where cyber threats are increasingly sophisticated and widespread, zone segmentation plays a vital role in building resilient and adaptable network architectures.

One of the primary benefits of zone segmentation is the principle of containment. By grouping similar systems and services into defined zones and controlling communication between them, an organization can prevent threats from spreading freely across the network. If an attacker gains access to a device in one zone, properly configured segmentation limits their ability to move laterally to more sensitive areas. This is particularly important for protecting critical assets such as databases, authentication servers, and intellectual property repositories. Without segmentation, a compromised endpoint could serve as a launching pad for further attacks throughout the entire organization, whereas with zone segmentation, the damage is more likely to be localized and manageable.

Improved policy enforcement is another significant advantage of zone segmentation. When networks are divided into zones with defined roles, administrators can apply tailored security policies that reflect the specific needs and risk profile of each zone. For example, a user zone may have broad internet access but limited internal access, while a data zone might be heavily restricted, allowing only specific services and authenticated users. This granularity ensures that access is not granted universally or arbitrarily but is aligned with business functions and security priorities. As a result, zone-based policies are not only more secure but also more aligned with how the organization operates.

Segmentation also supports better visibility and monitoring. When traffic is confined to defined zones and inter-zone communication is strictly controlled, it becomes easier to analyze network flows and detect anomalies. Security tools such as intrusion detection systems, firewalls, and logging mechanisms can be strategically placed at zone boundaries to monitor and inspect traffic. This placement ensures that all inter-zone traffic passes through control points where it can be analyzed and filtered. Suspicious behavior, such as unusual access attempts or unexpected data flows, is more likely to stand out when baseline behavior is confined to clearly defined paths. In this way, segmentation enhances both detection and response capabilities.

Another critical benefit is the facilitation of compliance with regulatory standards. Many industry regulations, including PCI DSS, HIPAA, and GDPR, require organizations to implement measures that limit access to sensitive data and ensure proper segmentation of systems. Zone segmentation provides a structured way to meet these requirements by isolating sensitive environments, controlling who can access them, and enforcing strong access policies. For example, a network that handles credit card transactions can isolate its cardholder data environment into a specific zone, limiting access only to authorized systems and personnel. This reduces the scope of compliance and simplifies audits, as the segmented environment is easier to document and validate against regulatory criteria.

Zone segmentation contributes significantly to operational efficiency. By separating services and functions into zones, organizations can reduce complexity and prevent conflicts between different types of traffic. For instance, separating voice-over-IP systems from general user traffic ensures that latency-sensitive communication is not disrupted by large file transfers or streaming media. Similarly, placing management systems in a separate zone allows for stricter access control and monitoring without affecting the performance of production systems. This logical organization of the network improves overall service quality, reduces troubleshooting time, and supports more efficient change management.

Segmentation is also essential for risk management. Not all assets within a network carry the same level of importance or vulnerability. By assigning systems to zones based on their criticality, organizations can allocate security resources more effectively. High-risk zones can be protected with additional controls such as multi-factor authentication, advanced threat detection, and data loss prevention technologies, while low-risk zones can operate with more basic safeguards. This risk-based approach ensures that security investments are focused where they are needed most, rather than being spread thin across the entire network.

In dynamic environments where networks evolve constantly, such as cloud infrastructure or virtualized data centers, zone segmentation provides flexibility and scalability. Virtual zones can be created and adjusted quickly to accommodate new services, users, or partners without compromising the security posture. As workloads shift and new applications are deployed, administrators can maintain control by assigning resources to appropriate zones and updating inter-zone policies accordingly. This adaptability is particularly important for supporting business agility and enabling innovation without introducing unnecessary risk.

Zone segmentation also simplifies incident response and recovery. When an incident occurs, such as a malware outbreak or a detected intrusion, segmentation limits the potential impact and makes it easier to isolate the affected systems. Response teams can focus their efforts within a specific zone, reducing the need to investigate or quarantine unrelated parts of the network. Furthermore, recovery actions such as restoring backups or reimaging systems can be conducted in a targeted manner, minimizing disruption to unaffected services. In this way, segmentation contributes to faster containment, lower costs, and reduced downtime during security incidents.

From an architectural perspective, zone segmentation introduces a modularity that aligns with best practices in design and engineering. Each zone becomes a self-contained unit with defined inputs, outputs, and controls. This modularity enables more predictable and consistent behavior, making it easier to test and validate network changes before they are deployed. It also supports layered security, or defense in depth, by placing multiple lines of defense between external threats and internal resources. Even if one control fails, the presence of zone boundaries ensures that additional protections remain in place to prevent or delay further compromise.

In complex organizations with multiple departments, partners, or client environments, zone segmentation allows for logical separation that supports multi-tenancy and data sovereignty. Different business units can operate in distinct zones, each with its own policies and governance structure. This isolation ensures that one department's systems and data do not interfere with or expose another's. In cases where external partners require access to internal resources, segmentation allows for tightly controlled and monitored access that limits the risk of exposure.

Overall, the benefits of zone segmentation extend far beyond simple traffic filtering. It enables organizations to implement structured, adaptive, and intelligent security measures that align with business objectives, technical realities, and regulatory obligations. Whether deployed in traditional networks, hybrid architectures, or cloud-native environments, zone segmentation remains one of the most effective strategies for reducing risk, increasing visibility, and maintaining control in a constantly evolving threat landscape. By thoughtfully applying this approach, organizations position themselves to respond confidently to challenges while maintaining the agility needed to compete and grow.

Configuring Zone Memberships

Configuring zone memberships is a critical step in the implementation of a zone-based firewall architecture. The effectiveness of zone-based policies and controls depends heavily on how accurately interfaces and network segments are assigned to their respective security zones. A zone membership determines which logical zone a physical or virtual interface belongs to, and this assignment directly influences the traffic that is permitted or denied between various parts of the network.

Without proper zone membership configuration, even the most well-planned firewall policies can fail to enforce security requirements or lead to unexpected behavior that disrupts legitimate communication. Understanding the principles, implications, and best practices of assigning zone memberships is essential for network administrators who aim to maintain a secure and manageable network environment.

The process begins with defining the zones themselves. A security zone represents a collection of interfaces or subnets that share a common security posture or trust level. These could include internal zones for trusted user devices, external zones for internet connectivity, DMZ zones for publicly accessible services, management zones for administrative access, and restricted zones for sensitive data or regulated systems. Once the zones are defined, each network interface on the firewall must be assigned to one of them. This membership is not just symbolic; it informs the firewall how to apply security policies to the traffic entering and leaving that interface. Assigning an interface to a zone essentially places the systems connected to that interface within the context of that zone's security policies.

When assigning interfaces to zones, administrators must have a clear understanding of the network topology and traffic flows. It is not enough to simply group interfaces based on geographic or physical proximity. Instead, the decision should be based on function, sensitivity, and communication requirements. For example, interfaces connected to user workstations might be assigned to a user zone, while those connecting to backend database servers belong to a data zone. Even within an internal network, different departments or business units may require separate zones to reflect distinct access privileges and risk levels. The objective is to align each interface with a zone that accurately reflects the security expectations for the connected systems.

In many network environments, especially those using VLANs, subinterfaces are created on physical interfaces to handle multiple logical networks. Each subinterface can be assigned to a different zone, allowing a single physical interface to serve multiple security contexts. This flexibility is particularly useful in environments where physical interface availability is limited or where virtual segmentation is used to separate traffic. By mapping each subinterface to the correct zone, administrators can maintain strong separation between different types of traffic without the need for additional hardware. However, this also introduces additional complexity, and care must be taken to ensure that each subinterface is correctly identified and associated with the appropriate zone.

A key principle in configuring zone memberships is that traffic between interfaces assigned to the same zone is typically unrestricted, while traffic between different zones is subject to firewall policy. This default behavior is both a strength and a potential vulnerability. It simplifies communication within zones and avoids the need for redundant rules, but it also means that overly broad or poorly defined zones can expose systems unnecessarily. For this reason, it is important to avoid assigning unrelated systems or services to the same zone simply for convenience. Each zone should represent a clearly defined trust boundary, and membership should be assigned with precision and purpose.

In addition to physical and logical interfaces, virtual interfaces used in VPN connections, tunnel interfaces, and loopback interfaces can also be assigned to zones. These virtual interfaces often serve as gateways for remote access or encrypted traffic and must be placed in zones that reflect the level of trust associated with their use. For instance, a VPN tunnel interface might be placed in a remote-access zone that is allowed limited connectivity to specific internal systems. Loopback interfaces, often used for management and routing purposes, might be placed in a dedicated management zone with strict access controls. Properly assigning these virtual interfaces ensures that all entry and exit points are accounted for within the zone-based security model.

Administrators must also consider the implications of reassigning zone memberships after initial configuration. Changing an interface's zone membership can have wide-ranging effects on existing security policies, potentially disrupting traffic flows or exposing systems to unfiltered communication. Before making such changes, it is important to conduct a thorough impact analysis, review dependent policies, and, if possible, test the changes in a controlled environment. Documentation should be updated to reflect the new configuration, and monitoring should be increased immediately following the change to detect any unintended consequences.

Consistency is another important factor in managing zone memberships. In large or multi-site networks, maintaining consistent zone assignments across devices helps ensure predictable behavior and simplifies policy management. This consistency can be achieved through templates, standardized naming conventions, and centralized configuration tools. When interfaces are consistently assigned to the same zones across different firewalls, it becomes easier to replicate policies, share logging and monitoring configurations, and maintain a coherent security posture across the entire network.

Zone membership configuration also plays a role in network troubleshooting. When access issues arise, one of the first steps is often to verify the zone membership of the interfaces involved. If an interface is not assigned to the expected zone, or if a device is connected to the wrong interface, the firewall may apply incorrect policies or drop traffic altogether. Administrators must be able to quickly identify zone assignments and understand their impact on policy enforcement. Tools that visualize zone relationships and interface mappings can greatly aid in this process, reducing the time needed to diagnose and resolve issues.

As networks evolve, so too must the zone membership configuration. New devices, services, or organizational changes may necessitate the creation of new zones or the reassignment of existing interfaces. It is essential that zone design and membership assignments remain flexible and adaptable while continuing to uphold the principles of least privilege, segmentation, and clarity. Ongoing evaluation of zone assignments ensures that they continue to reflect the current operational and security landscape.

Configuring zone memberships is not just a technical task but a strategic one. It defines how the firewall perceives and manages different parts of the network, and it lays the foundation for the enforcement of security policies. Through thoughtful and deliberate assignment of interfaces to zones, administrators can build a robust framework for traffic control, threat containment, and policy enforcement. This framework supports not only immediate security goals but also the long-term scalability and maintainability of the network. By investing the necessary attention to detail and alignment with organizational objectives, configuring zone memberships becomes a powerful tool in the overall defense strategy of any modern enterprise.

Inter-Zone Traffic Control

Inter-zone traffic control is a fundamental aspect of modern network security, governing how data moves between different security zones within a network architecture. As networks become more complex, with a wide range of users, devices, applications, and services distributed across various segments, controlling the flow of traffic between these segments becomes a critical defense mechanism. The core principle behind inter-zone traffic control is that not all parts of a network are equally trusted or equally vulnerable. Different zones are created to reflect different levels of trust, sensitivity, and function. The policies that regulate communication between these zones determine the degree of separation and the level of scrutiny applied to traffic as it crosses zone boundaries.

A well-designed inter-zone traffic control strategy begins with a clear understanding of the zones in question. Each zone should represent a distinct security context. For example, an internal zone may consist of employee workstations, a data zone may house critical databases and storage systems, a management zone may include network infrastructure and administrative tools, and an external zone may face the internet or external partners. Between these zones, firewalls and other security devices act as gatekeepers, enforcing policies that dictate what types of communication are permitted, under what conditions, and with what level of inspection.

One of the most important characteristics of inter-zone traffic control is the default deny posture. In most zone-based firewall configurations, traffic between zones is blocked by default unless explicitly allowed by policy. This conservative approach ensures that access is only granted where there is a defined need, thereby reducing the risk of unauthorized access and lateral movement within the network. For traffic to be permitted between two zones, administrators must create a policy that specifies the source zone, destination zone, protocols, ports, and, in some cases, user identity or application type. This level of specificity provides granular control and enforces the principle of least privilege.

Policies governing inter-zone traffic are often based on business requirements. For example, users in the internal zone may need to access web applications hosted in the DMZ zone, or database servers in the data zone may need to synchronize with remote backup services through a secure connection to the external zone. Each of these scenarios requires careful consideration of which traffic should be allowed and which should be blocked. The policies must be crafted to permit necessary functions while denying all other traffic. This balance requires an in-depth understanding of application behavior, protocol dependencies, and user workflows to ensure that legitimate activity is not inadvertently disrupted.

Application awareness adds an important dimension to inter-zone traffic control. Traditional policies based solely on IP addresses and ports may not provide sufficient protection in environments where applications use dynamic ports, tunneling, or encryption to evade detection. Next-generation firewalls enhance inter-zone controls by inspecting the content of traffic at higher layers of the OSI model. This allows them to identify specific applications, even when they are running over standard ports such as HTTPS. With this capability, policies can be written to allow or deny traffic based on the actual application in use, not just the transport protocol, enabling more precise enforcement and reducing the risk of disguised threats passing through allowed ports.

Logging and monitoring are essential components of inter-zone traffic control. Every policy decision should be accompanied by visibility into the traffic it permits or blocks. Security teams rely on logs to understand which connections are being attempted, which are succeeding or failing, and whether those patterns indicate normal business operations or potential security incidents. Logs from inter-zone traffic can reveal misconfigurations, unauthorized access attempts, or signs of compromise. This information is critical for ongoing security assessments, incident response, and compliance reporting. It also provides the feedback loop necessary to fine-tune policies and adjust zone boundaries as the network evolves.

Inter-zone policies must also account for special cases, such as encrypted traffic and VPN connections. When data is encrypted, traditional inspection methods may not be able to verify the contents of the traffic. In these cases, policies may need to include SSL decryption capabilities at the firewall or enforce strict control over which endpoints are permitted to initiate encrypted sessions. VPN connections introduce a new dimension to inter-zone traffic, as they often bridge remote users or external partners directly into internal zones. To mitigate the associated risks, VPN endpoints should be placed in isolated zones with tightly controlled access to the rest of the network, and inter-zone policies should reflect the minimum level of access required for the intended functions.

Performance is another consideration in inter-zone traffic control. As traffic passes through policy enforcement points, each packet must be evaluated against a set of rules. In high-throughput environments, poorly optimized policies or overly complex inspection rules can introduce latency or reduce network performance. To address this, administrators must prioritize rule order, eliminate redundancies, and ensure that the most frequently matched rules are processed efficiently. Many firewall platforms offer tools to simulate policy impact or analyze rule utilization, helping to maintain optimal performance without compromising security.

Scalability is a growing concern as organizations adopt hybrid cloud, multi-cloud, and software-defined networking architectures. In these dynamic environments, inter-zone traffic control must adapt to constantly changing endpoints, elastic workloads, and automated provisioning systems. Static IP-based policies may no longer be effective or sustainable. Instead, security policies should leverage tags, roles, or service identifiers to define access rules. This approach allows policies to be applied consistently, even as resources move or scale. It also facilitates centralized policy management across multiple platforms, ensuring uniform enforcement of security controls regardless of where traffic originates or terminates.

Finally, inter-zone traffic control must be viewed as an ongoing process rather than a one-time configuration task. As business needs evolve, new applications are deployed, and threats change, policies must be reviewed and updated regularly. This includes evaluating existing rules for relevance, tightening overly permissive access, and retiring rules that are no longer needed. Policy reviews should involve collaboration between network, security, and application teams to ensure that controls remain aligned with operational goals and risk tolerance. In complex networks, change management procedures and policy versioning help maintain consistency and accountability, preventing unintended disruptions or security regressions.

Inter-zone traffic control is the backbone of secure network segmentation. By carefully defining how different areas of the network interact, organizations can reduce their exposure to threats, enforce data protection requirements, and maintain control over communication paths. It allows for a structured and disciplined approach to network access, supporting both security and operational objectives. When implemented with precision, monitored diligently, and adjusted proactively, inter-zone traffic control provides a resilient and adaptive framework for defending against today's ever-evolving cyber threats.

Creating Zone Policies

Creating zone policies is one of the most important tasks in a zone-based firewall architecture. These policies dictate how traffic is allowed to flow between defined security zones, and they serve as the central enforcement mechanism for organizational access control. A zone policy is essentially a set of rules that explicitly state what type of communication is permitted or denied between two specific zones. The development of these policies must be guided by a deep understanding of business requirements, application behavior, security objectives, and network topology. When constructed carefully and logically, zone policies form a robust security framework that controls data flow, minimizes risk, and ensures operational continuity across diverse systems and users.

The first step in creating effective zone policies is identifying all zone relationships within the network. This involves mapping out every security zone and analyzing which zones need to communicate with one another. Not every zone will or should communicate with all others. For example, user workstations in a general-purpose internal zone may require access to web servers in a DMZ zone but should have no direct access to database servers in a secure data zone. Similarly, administrative systems in a management zone may need access to all other zones for monitoring and configuration purposes, but access should be unidirectional and restricted to specific protocols and ports. The key is to establish a clear and justified communication matrix that outlines permissible inter-zone connections and the specific contexts in which they are allowed.

Once the required zone interactions are identified, the next step is to define the criteria for allowing or denying traffic. This includes specifying source and destination zones, protocols, source and destination IP addresses or subnets, and port numbers. In more advanced environments, policies may also include conditions based on user identity, time of day, application type, or threat detection status. Each rule within a zone policy should have a clear business justification. If the reason for allowing a certain type of traffic cannot be articulated, it is a strong indication that the rule may be unnecessary or potentially risky. The process of rule creation should involve collaboration between network engineers, system administrators, application owners, and security teams to ensure that policies reflect real-world requirements without exposing the network to excessive risk.

Granularity is critical when writing zone policies. Broad, overly permissive rules can create significant vulnerabilities by allowing unnecessary access between zones. For example, a policy that allows all TCP traffic from a user zone to a server zone might permit applications that are not officially supported or secure. Instead, rules should be as specific as possible, allowing only the required traffic. A good example would be a rule that permits HTTPS traffic from a subnet in the user zone to a specific server IP in the application zone, using port 443 only. This minimizes exposure and limits the potential damage that could occur if an endpoint were compromised. Fine-tuned policies reduce the attack surface and make it easier to detect anomalies in traffic behavior.

Another important consideration when creating zone policies is the directionality of communication. Policies must specify not only what type of traffic is allowed but also in which direction it is permitted to flow. A policy that allows traffic from the internal zone to the DMZ might be acceptable, but allowing unsolicited inbound traffic from the DMZ to the internal zone is usually a serious security risk. Unidirectional policies enforce a controlled flow of information and ensure that only the intended initiator of a session can communicate. In scenarios where bidirectional communication is necessary, such as in replication or synchronization between two data centers, additional safeguards must be put in place to verify traffic legitimacy and prevent misuse.

Logging and auditing should be embedded into the policy creation process. For each rule, administrators should decide whether it is necessary to generate a log entry when the rule is matched. Logging helps track the use of each policy and provides valuable data for monitoring and incident response. Especially for deny rules, logging can help identify attempts to access unauthorized services or zones. These logs become even more critical during forensic investigations, audits, and compliance checks, as they provide a traceable history of inter-zone communications. When combined with centralized logging and SIEM systems, zone policy logs contribute to a comprehensive picture of the organization's security posture.

Policy testing and validation are also crucial steps before deploying new zone policies into a production environment. A policy that looks correct on paper may have unintended consequences when applied, such as blocking legitimate traffic or permitting unauthorized access. It is essential to simulate policy behavior, test rules in a controlled setting, and review logs for unexpected matches or anomalies. Many firewalls support rule simulation or shadow policies, which allow administrators to evaluate the impact of a rule without enforcing it. This capability can be used to validate proposed policies before they are committed and to identify overlaps, redundancies, or conflicts in existing rules.

As zone policies grow in number and complexity, it becomes increasingly important to maintain documentation and use a consistent naming convention. Each policy should be documented with a description of its purpose, the systems it affects, and the stakeholders responsible for maintaining it. This documentation aids in change management, troubleshooting, and audits. Clear names for policies and rules, such as "Allow_HTTP_Internal_to_DMZ_Web," make it easier to understand their intent and facilitate team collaboration. Without such discipline, policies can become unmanageable over time, increasing the risk of misconfiguration or accidental exposure.

Ongoing maintenance is a fundamental part of effective zone policy management. Policies should be reviewed regularly to ensure they are still necessary and appropriate. Changes in application architecture, business processes, or regulatory requirements may render some rules obsolete or require adjustments. Periodic policy audits help identify unused rules, overly broad permissions, and outdated configurations. These reviews should be formalized within the organization's change management and security governance frameworks to ensure accountability and consistency. In addition, a feedback loop should be in place so that incidents, anomalies, and user feedback can lead to policy improvements.

Creating zone policies is not just a technical function but a strategic process that bridges IT security and business operations. It requires careful planning, precision, and ongoing collaboration between different teams. By aligning policies with organizational goals, risk tolerance, and real-world usage patterns, administrators can build a policy framework that is both secure and functional. A well-constructed set of zone policies enables robust control over network traffic, supports compliance efforts, and forms the backbone of a resilient, well-segmented security architecture. The strength of any zone-based firewall deployment ultimately depends on the quality and clarity of the policies that govern it, making their creation a task of critical importance.

Using Zones for Attack Mitigation

Using security zones for attack mitigation is a strategic and highly effective approach in modern network defense. The core idea behind this methodology is to divide the network into multiple logical segments or zones based on the level of trust, sensitivity, or function of the systems within them. Once zones are defined, administrators can enforce granular security controls and monitor traffic that crosses these boundaries. When properly implemented, this segmentation acts as a series of containment layers that help prevent the spread of attacks, detect malicious behavior early, and apply tailored responses based on the nature of each zone. As cyber threats continue to evolve in complexity and frequency, zone-based mitigation strategies offer resilience and control in the face of an ever-changing threat landscape.

One of the most fundamental benefits of using zones for attack mitigation is the ability to isolate threats. In a flat network where all devices can freely communicate, a single compromised system can become a launchpad for widespread attacks, moving laterally through the network without encountering resistance. By contrast, in a zone-based architecture, lateral movement is hindered by clearly defined boundaries and enforcement policies. If a system within a user zone is infected with malware, for example, the infection is far less likely to reach critical systems housed in the data zone or management zone. Each attempted movement between zones must comply with predefined rules, and unauthorized communication is blocked automatically. This drastically reduces the potential blast radius of any breach and buys valuable time for detection and response.

Another advantage of using zones for mitigation is the enhanced visibility it provides. Each boundary between zones serves as a checkpoint where traffic can be inspected, logged, and analyzed. By monitoring these inter-zone transitions, security teams can identify patterns that deviate from normal behavior. Suspicious spikes in traffic, unexpected protocol usage, or unusual access attempts can be flagged for investigation. Zones enable more targeted monitoring by narrowing the scope of what is considered normal or abnormal in each context. For instance, the communication expected between a web application in the DMZ and a backend server in the internal zone is well-defined and predictable. Any deviation from this baseline can trigger alerts, helping to identify an attack in progress before significant damage occurs.

Zones also support the implementation of differentiated controls based on risk and sensitivity. Not all systems face the same level of threat or require the same level of protection. A zone that includes public-facing services, such as a web server or email gateway, will be exposed to a higher volume and variety of attacks than an isolated zone housing sensitive financial records. By assigning these systems to separate zones, administrators can apply more aggressive inspection, filtering, and rate-limiting to higher-risk zones without imposing the same overhead on zones where traffic is more trusted. This allows security measures to be applied intelligently and efficiently, focusing resources where they are most needed.

A powerful example of zone-based attack mitigation is the use of quarantine or remediation zones. When a device is suspected of being compromised, it can be automatically moved or reclassified into a special quarantine zone. In this zone, the device's access to the rest of the network is severely restricted, and it can only communicate with designated remediation systems or security analysts. This containment allows the threat to be neutralized without disrupting the entire network or immediately removing the device from service. Automated tools and endpoint detection systems can integrate with firewalls and network access control platforms to enforce this isolation dynamically, ensuring a rapid response that limits attacker mobility and prevents further compromise.

Zones also facilitate more secure onboarding and offboarding of systems and users. When a new device connects to the network, whether it belongs to an employee, guest, or third-party contractor, it can initially be placed in a low-trust or guest zone. From there, additional authentication, compliance checks, or endpoint assessments can determine whether the device should be granted access to more trusted zones. This approach ensures that only verified, compliant devices gain access to sensitive resources, and it helps prevent unauthorized devices from acting as entry points for attackers. Similarly, when a device or user no longer requires access, their removal from the higher-trust zones is simplified and enforced by the same segmentation policies.

In distributed and cloud-connected environments, zone-based mitigation strategies remain effective and adaptable. Whether resources are on-premises, in a private cloud, or part of a public cloud service, the concept of logical zones still applies. Virtual networks, security groups, and cloud firewalls allow administrators to replicate zone boundaries and enforce policies consistently across multiple platforms. This continuity is essential in hybrid environments, where traffic often moves between cloud and on-prem systems. By extending zone concepts across these domains, organizations can maintain visibility, apply consistent controls, and prevent gaps that attackers might exploit during transitions.

Another area where zone-based strategies shine is in defending against distributed denial of service (DDoS) attacks. When a network is segmented into zones, it becomes easier to identify the source and target of unusual traffic volumes. Edge zones that interface with the internet can be equipped with traffic scrubbing services and rate-limiting rules that mitigate the impact of volumetric attacks before they reach internal systems. In the event of a sustained attack, administrators can reroute, throttle, or block traffic to specific zones without affecting internal operations. This ability to isolate and absorb the effects of external attacks protects the integrity of critical systems and maintains operational availability.

Zones also enable better response coordination during a security incident. When an alert is triggered, analysts can quickly determine which zones are involved and what types of communication are affected. This zoning context allows for more precise response actions, such as disabling specific policies, reassigning zone memberships, or escalating monitoring on certain boundaries. Because each zone has a clearly defined role and set of communication rules, the process of triage and containment becomes more structured and less prone to error. This structured response is essential in time-sensitive situations, where rapid decision-making can make the difference between a contained incident and a widespread breach.

In complex enterprise environments with hundreds or thousands of interconnected systems, the use of security zones is not merely a best practice but a necessity. Attackers are constantly searching for weak links, misconfigured systems, and opportunities to exploit implicit trust. Zones counter this by enforcing explicit boundaries, scrutinizing every inter-zone request, and applying policies that are rooted in risk management and operational logic. They turn a chaotic landscape into an organized battlefield where defenses are layered, coordinated, and adaptive.

Using zones for attack mitigation transforms network security from a reactive process into a proactive strategy. It creates defensive depth, restricts attacker movement, enhances detection capabilities, and supports faster, more targeted incident response. When zones are designed thoughtfully and enforced rigorously, they become more than just a configuration—they become an integral part of the organization's security posture. As threats continue to grow in sophistication and scope, leveraging zone-based architectures will remain one of the most effective ways to keep networks secure, resilient, and under control.

Advanced Zone Architecture Designs

Advanced zone architecture designs represent the evolution of traditional network segmentation strategies into highly dynamic, scalable, and context-aware systems that address the increasing complexity of modern enterprise networks. These architectures go beyond the basic separation of trusted and untrusted zones, introducing multilayered segmentation, microsegmentation, service-specific zones, and dynamic zoning mechanisms that adapt to changing workloads, threats, and user contexts. The primary goal of advanced zone architecture is to strengthen security while maintaining the flexibility and agility required by contemporary IT environments, including hybrid clouds, remote access models, and decentralized infrastructures.

One of the defining characteristics of advanced zone design is the use of multilayered segmentation. Instead of relying on broad zones such as internal, DMZ, and external, multilayered architectures introduce a hierarchy of zones that reflect finer distinctions between systems and their roles. For example, within an internal network, an organization might implement separate zones for end-user workstations, application servers, file storage, authentication systems, and network management tools. Each of these zones would have tailored access controls and policies that define how they interact with one another. This hierarchical design enhances security by reducing the impact radius of a potential breach. If an attacker gains access to a workstation, they must overcome multiple zone boundaries and policy checkpoints to reach sensitive backend systems.

Microsegmentation is another core feature of advanced zone architectures. It involves the creation of very small, granular security zones—often down to the level of individual workloads or applications. Microsegmentation is typically enforced through software-defined networking (SDN), host-based firewalls, or virtual security appliances. In such environments, policies are written not just between physical network segments but between virtual machines, containers, or processes. This allows for extremely precise control over east-west traffic, which refers to data moving laterally within the network. By isolating workloads even within the same physical infrastructure, microsegmentation prevents lateral movement by attackers and minimizes the risk posed by compromised systems or insider threats.

Advanced architectures also incorporate context-aware zoning. Traditional zones are defined based on static criteria such as IP addresses or physical interfaces. In contrast, context-aware zoning uses dynamic attributes like user identity, device posture, location, and real-time threat intelligence to determine zone membership and access privileges. This model supports dynamic security postures that adjust according to changing conditions. For example, a user connecting from a corporate laptop during business hours may be assigned to a trusted zone with broad access, while the same user connecting from an unmanaged device at night may be placed in a restricted zone with limited permissions. This adaptability supports the principles of zero trust and conditional access, both of which are essential for defending against modern threats.

Service-specific zoning is another refinement found in advanced architectures. Rather than grouping systems solely by function or trust level, zones can be defined around specific services or application stacks. For instance, a healthcare organization might create separate zones for electronic health record systems, medical imaging platforms, and patient-facing portals. Each zone would include all the components needed to deliver a particular service, and inter-zone policies would govern how services interact. This approach aligns security architecture with business services, making it easier to manage dependencies, enforce compliance, and isolate issues when they arise.

Service-specific zoning also supports high availability and disaster recovery planning by ensuring that critical services are self-contained and resilient.

Automation plays a significant role in advanced zone architecture. Manual management of complex zone configurations and policy sets is both error-prone and time-consuming. Automation tools allow for the dynamic assignment of zone memberships, the real-time enforcement of policies, and the orchestration of security responses. When integrated with configuration management systems, identity and access management platforms, and threat detection tools, automation can adapt zone configurations based on predefined rules or detected anomalies. For example, if an endpoint is flagged for suspicious behavior, it can automatically be moved into a quarantine zone, and specific alerts and restrictions can be applied. Automation reduces response times and ensures consistent enforcement of security policies across diverse and distributed environments.

Another emerging trend in advanced zone architecture is the integration of network and application layer controls. While traditional zoning is often limited to network-layer boundaries, modern architectures combine network segmentation with application-layer inspection, behavioral analysis, and policy enforcement. This convergence is made possible through next-generation firewalls, deep packet inspection tools, and advanced security platforms that operate across multiple OSI layers. It allows for unified control over who can access what, from where, using which application, and under what circumstances. This level of integration is critical for defending against application-layer attacks, data exfiltration, and sophisticated multi-vector threats.

Cloud-native zone architectures offer further innovation by leveraging the capabilities of cloud service providers to implement segmentation at scale. Public clouds such as AWS, Azure, and Google Cloud allow administrators to create virtual networks, security groups, network access control lists, and identity-based policies that mirror the functions of traditional zones. In these environments, segmentation can be applied to serverless functions, containers, managed services, and even SaaS applications. Cross-account or cross-region policies can be managed centrally through infrastructure as code tools and cloud-native security platforms. The elasticity and global distribution of cloud resources require zone architectures that are equally flexible, scalable, and resilient.

Hybrid and multi-cloud deployments introduce additional complexity that advanced zone architecture must accommodate. Segmentation must span on-premises systems, private clouds, and multiple public cloud platforms. This demands a unified policy model that can interpret and enforce access controls regardless of the underlying infrastructure. Solutions such as secure access service edge (SASE), software-defined WAN (SD-WAN), and cloud access security brokers (CASBs) help bridge these gaps by abstracting policy enforcement from the physical topology. Advanced architectures in such scenarios rely on centralized visibility, consistent policy enforcement, and real-time adaptation to maintain security across all zones, regardless of where data or users reside.

Advanced zone architecture also benefits from comprehensive logging, telemetry, and analytics. By capturing detailed data on traffic flows, policy matches, and inter-zone communication, administrators gain a holistic view of how the network operates and where anomalies may be occurring. Security information and event management (SIEM) systems, along with machine learning-based analytics platforms, can detect patterns that signal potential threats or misconfigurations. Insights derived from this data feed back into the architecture, allowing for continuous improvement and more intelligent zoning decisions. In highly regulated industries, this visibility is also essential for demonstrating compliance and maintaining audit readiness.

Ultimately, advanced zone architecture designs are a response to the need for greater security, agility, and visibility in modern networks. They transform segmentation from a static configuration into a dynamic, intelligent framework capable of defending against a wide array of threats. By combining fine-grained control, automation, context-awareness, and cloud-native capabilities, these designs empower organizations to implement robust security measures without compromising operational efficiency. As digital infrastructures continue to expand and diversify, advanced zone architectures will remain a cornerstone of effective cybersecurity strategy, enabling organizations to meet new challenges with confidence and control.

Bridging ACLs and Zones for Control

Bridging Access Control Lists and security zones represents a powerful strategy for achieving granular control over network traffic while maintaining the benefits of structured segmentation. Traditionally, ACLs and zones have served as distinct mechanisms in network security: ACLs function as packet-level filters applied at interfaces, while zones provide a logical grouping of interfaces based on trust or function, enabling policies to govern inter-zone communication. When used together effectively, these two mechanisms complement each other to create a layered defense model that is both flexible and enforceable. Combining the precision of ACLs with the organization of zone-based architecture allows security administrators to fine-tune permissions and enforce contextual security in a more manageable and scalable way.

One of the primary challenges in managing network traffic is achieving the balance between broad policies that are easy to administer and specific rules that meet complex security requirements. Zones simplify administration by grouping interfaces and applying policies between those groups, reducing the need for configuring rules on each individual interface. However, zones alone may not provide the granularity needed to control traffic between specific hosts or services within the same or different zones. This is where ACLs add value. By applying ACLs at the interface level, administrators can write rules that apply to particular IP addresses, subnets, ports, or protocols, refining what is permitted or denied even within the boundaries established by zone policies.

For example, consider a scenario in which a zone policy permits communication from the internal zone to the DMZ zone for web services. While this broad policy allows HTTP and HTTPS traffic, an ACL can be applied on the internal zone's interface to limit that permission only to a specific internal subnet or to a particular server. The ACL can define the source and destination IP addresses and ports, allowing only necessary traffic to flow. This dual-layer approach ensures that even if a zone policy is permissive by necessity, specific ACLs can restrict access in a targeted and precise manner. It's a form of defense-in-depth that offers both the manageability of zones and the specificity of ACLs.

In some network environments, the reliance on ACLs is necessary due to legacy systems or hardware that does not support full zone-based policies. In these cases, integrating ACLs with existing zone architecture provides a transitional path toward a more modern security posture. ACLs can enforce restrictions while the infrastructure is incrementally migrated toward a zone-based model. Even in fully zone-aware environments, ACLs serve as a fine-tuning tool, allowing administrators to handle exceptions and apply unique rules that are too detailed or context-specific for zone policies alone.

The integration of ACLs and zones requires careful planning and documentation. Each ACL must be reviewed in the context of the zone policies it intersects. Redundancies should be avoided, and conflicts must be identified to prevent inconsistent behavior. For instance, a zone policy may allow all traffic between two zones, but an ACL might deny specific traffic types at the interface. Without proper documentation, such overlaps can result in confusion, troubleshooting difficulties, and unintended service disruptions. Therefore, clear documentation that maps out both zone policies and interface-level ACLs is essential for maintaining clarity and ensuring that all access controls align with organizational security requirements.

Monitoring is also a crucial aspect of bridging ACLs and zones. Logs from both zone policy matches and ACL rule hits should be collected and analyzed to understand traffic flows and identify anomalies. Modern network devices and firewalls often provide logging options for both types of control, and these logs should be integrated into a centralized system such as a SIEM platform. Correlating logs from ACLs and zones can reveal misconfigurations, unused rules, or attempts to bypass controls. This visibility enables administrators to refine their controls continuously and ensures that the integrated system remains aligned with the intended security posture.

Scalability is another consideration when combining ACLs and zones. As networks grow, the number of ACL entries and zone relationships can expand rapidly, potentially leading to management overhead. To address this, many organizations adopt policy templates or automation frameworks that can generate and apply both zone policies and ACLs based on predefined criteria. This approach not only reduces the potential for human error but also ensures consistency across devices and environments. For example, a network automation tool can apply ACLs to all access-layer switches to restrict certain traffic types, while simultaneously updating zone policies on core firewalls to reflect broader trust relationships.

Using ACLs within zones also provides benefits for temporary access requirements. In situations where a temporary connection is needed—such as for maintenance, testing, or third-party access—an ACL can be deployed quickly on an interface to allow the specific traffic, without the need to alter the more permanent zone policies. Once the access window is closed, the ACL can be removed, reverting the system to its previous state. This method avoids the risk of introducing long-term policy exceptions into zone configurations and supports better control over temporary permissions.

Another use case for bridging ACLs and zones involves multi-tenant or multi-departmental environments, where different groups share infrastructure but require isolated policies. While zones may define high-level separation between tenants, ACLs can enforce additional boundaries within those zones, ensuring that users from one department cannot reach specific services or devices belonging to another. This layered control supports compliance, confidentiality, and the enforcement of service-level agreements. In shared cloud or virtualized infrastructures, this method becomes especially valuable, as virtual interfaces and logical zoning may not provide sufficient granularity on their own.

The synergy between ACLs and zones extends to advanced use cases such as policy-based routing, QoS enforcement, and application-aware filtering. An ACL can identify specific traffic and apply tags that influence routing decisions or service levels, while the zone-based firewall evaluates whether the traffic should be allowed between zones. This dual approach ensures that traffic is not only allowed but also treated appropriately based on its characteristics and the context in which it is flowing. In security terms, it provides both a gatekeeper and a traffic cop, each playing a distinct but complementary role in ensuring that communication is safe, efficient, and appropriate.

Bridging ACLs and zones is a strategy that combines the best of both worlds: the structure and clarity of zone-based segmentation with the detailed control offered by ACLs. This approach allows organizations to implement highly adaptable and granular security policies while maintaining scalability and operational efficiency. It recognizes that no single method of access control is sufficient in isolation and leverages the strengths of each to build a comprehensive and resilient security posture. As networks continue to grow in complexity, the ability to blend different layers of control effectively becomes not only beneficial but essential for protecting assets, ensuring compliance, and enabling secure business operations.

Introduction to Context-Based Access Control (CBAC)

Context-Based Access Control, commonly referred to as CBAC, is a dynamic traffic filtering mechanism that enhances traditional access control models by evaluating not only static rules but also the context in which connections occur. It provides a more intelligent and adaptive form of traffic inspection by analyzing the state and characteristics of traffic flows, rather than simply relying on static source and destination IP addresses or port numbers. This contextual awareness allows CBAC to make access control decisions based on the behavior of traffic over time, effectively bringing stateful inspection into environments that previously depended on static ACLs. The introduction of CBAC represented a major leap forward in network security by enabling devices such as routers and firewalls to understand and manage the lifecycle of traffic sessions.

The fundamental principle behind CBAC is statefulness. Unlike standard access control mechanisms that apply rules uniformly to all packets regardless of their origin or purpose, CBAC tracks the state of each session passing through the network device. It observes the initiation of a connection, the maintenance of that connection, and its eventual termination. This means that traffic related to an established session can be allowed through automatically, while unrelated or unsolicited traffic is denied. For instance, when a user from the internal network initiates an outbound HTTP connection to a website, CBAC inspects the initial request, recognizes the establishment of a session, and dynamically creates temporary access rules to allow the returning HTTP response traffic. These rules are not permanent; they are removed once the session ends or after a predefined timeout period, significantly reducing the window of opportunity for malicious use.

One of the key advantages of CBAC is its ability to provide dynamic access control without requiring complex and static configurations. In a traditional ACL-based setup, administrators would need to create rules for both outbound and inbound traffic, including anticipating all possible legitimate responses from external servers. This can lead to overly permissive rules, creating unnecessary security risks. CBAC eliminates this challenge by automatically allowing return traffic that corresponds to verified outbound sessions, while still blocking all other unsolicited inbound traffic. This capability brings a balance of security and functionality, as users can interact with external services without administrators needing to open wide, permanent channels through the firewall or router.

CBAC also offers deep packet inspection capabilities. It does not merely inspect packet headers for IP address and port information; it can analyze the payload of packets to understand the application-layer behavior. This means it can inspect protocols like HTTP, FTP, DNS, and SIP, tracking how these protocols operate and recognizing patterns that signify legitimate versus potentially malicious activity. For example, CBAC can track FTP control connections and dynamically open ports for the corresponding data channels, something that cannot be easily achieved with static ACLs. This application-layer awareness allows CBAC to handle complex protocols that use multiple ports or establish connections dynamically, offering greater compatibility and security for modern applications.

Another important feature of CBAC is its integration with alerting and logging mechanisms. As CBAC monitors and filters traffic, it can generate detailed logs that provide visibility into session activity, policy matches, and potential security incidents. These logs can be sent to centralized monitoring systems, helping administrators detect anomalies and assess the impact of policy changes. Real-time alerting allows security teams to respond quickly to suspicious behavior, such as unexpected connection attempts, protocol misuse, or high session counts that might indicate a denial-of-service attempt. Logging also supports auditing and compliance by documenting how access control policies are enforced and how traffic is managed dynamically across the network.

In terms of implementation, CBAC is typically deployed on network routers and firewalls, particularly those running Cisco IOS, which originally popularized the technology. Administrators define inspection rules for specific traffic types, and the device begins tracking and managing sessions accordingly. CBAC can be configured to inspect multiple protocols, apply different timeout values based on traffic type, and enforce per-session limits to prevent abuse. These configuration options allow for a tailored approach that aligns with organizational policies and operational needs. Moreover, CBAC can work alongside static ACLs, with ACLs providing baseline controls and CBAC offering dynamic enhancements based on real-time traffic analysis.

Security policies enforced by CBAC are inherently more adaptive and resilient than those based purely on static configurations. The stateful nature of CBAC makes it especially effective at handling attacks that exploit the statelessness of traditional ACLs. For instance, CBAC can help prevent spoofing attacks, where an attacker sends packets with a forged source address, by verifying that all traffic corresponds to a valid session. It can also detect and block attempts to bypass security by using non-standard ports or fragmented packets, since CBAC inspects not just the individual packets but the entire session behavior. This contextual inspection provides a much richer security posture that can adapt to evolving threats.

As organizations continue to adopt cloud services, support remote users, and implement complex application architectures, the need for intelligent access control mechanisms like CBAC grows. Static firewall rules cannot keep pace with the fluid nature of modern traffic, especially when services are dynamically provisioned, applications span multiple layers, and threats come from both internal and external sources. CBAC's ability to dynamically manage access, based on real-time session information and deep protocol understanding, makes it a valuable tool in building secure, flexible networks.

CBAC also aligns well with the principles of zero trust and microsegmentation. In a zero-trust model, every session must be authenticated and authorized based on contextual factors. CBAC supports this model by treating each connection individually, ensuring that only verified sessions are allowed to continue and that all others are denied by default. Similarly, in microsegmented networks, where fine-grained control is applied to traffic within the internal environment, CBAC can enforce per-session inspection and control, preventing lateral movement of threats and ensuring that even internal traffic is subject to scrutiny.

In practice, deploying CBAC requires thoughtful planning and tuning. Administrators must select which protocols to inspect, define reasonable timeouts, and determine session limits to avoid performance degradation. They must also ensure that inspection rules do not interfere with legitimate traffic or introduce unnecessary latency. Regular monitoring, testing, and policy refinement are essential to maintain a balance between security and usability. When implemented properly, CBAC becomes a powerful layer of dynamic defense that complements static controls and supports a robust, adaptive security architecture capable of withstanding the pressures of a constantly changing threat environment.

How CBAC Works

Context-Based Access Control, or CBAC, operates as a dynamic and stateful traffic inspection mechanism that allows routers and firewalls to intelligently manage network access based on the actual context of network sessions. Unlike static access control lists that permit or deny traffic solely based on predefined rules tied to IP addresses, protocols, and ports, CBAC dynamically learns and reacts to the traffic it sees. It does so by inspecting and tracking the state of traffic sessions as they are established, maintained, and terminated. CBAC fundamentally changes how access is granted, making decisions based on the legitimacy of a session rather than simply trusting the characteristics of individual packets. This process greatly enhances the security posture of any network by ensuring that only validated traffic flows are allowed, particularly for inbound sessions that could otherwise represent significant risks.

The operation of CBAC begins when traffic is initiated from an internal network toward an external destination. As the internal device sends a request—for example, a web browser reaching out to an external website over HTTP—CBAC inspects this outbound traffic at the configured firewall or router interface. When CBAC is enabled, the router or firewall analyzes the request and identifies critical information about the session, including source and destination IP addresses, source and destination ports, and the protocol in use. It then creates a stateful entry in a dynamic session table that records this information and marks the session as established. This entry becomes the basis for evaluating any return traffic that is associated with the session.

Once the session is initiated and recorded, CBAC monitors incoming traffic from the external source and compares it to the session table. If a packet arrives that matches an existing session entry, CBAC allows it through. This return traffic may be a web server sending the requested web page to the internal client, and because it is part of a previously inspected and authorized session, it is considered legitimate. However, if any traffic arrives at the CBAC-enabled interface that does not match a valid session entry, it is dropped. This protects the network from unsolicited or malicious inbound connections, such as port scans, random probes, or unsolicited data packets that are not part of a recognized session. By using this stateful inspection approach, CBAC provides a much more secure alternative to traditional stateless packet filters.

CBAC is not limited to basic protocols such as HTTP or DNS. It supports inspection of several complex, multi-channel protocols including FTP, H.323, and SIP. These protocols often require dynamic port assignments or involve separate control and data channels. In a traditional firewall configuration, it would be necessary to statically open all potential ports that a protocol might use, which could expose the network to unnecessary risks. CBAC, on the other hand, understands how these protocols operate and can dynamically permit the required ports for the duration of the session. For example, in the case of FTP, CBAC inspects the control connection to determine which ports will be used for the data transfer, and it temporarily opens those ports only for that session. Once the session ends or times out, CBAC closes the ports, preventing any further use.

Another critical component of CBAC is the timeout mechanism. Each session entry maintained by CBAC has a timeout value associated with it. If a session remains idle for longer than the configured timeout period, CBAC assumes the session is no longer active and removes it from the table. This mechanism helps reduce the consumption of system resources and ensures that temporary permissions are not left open indefinitely. Administrators can configure different timeout values for different protocols, providing flexibility based on the behavior and expected lifespan of sessions. For example, HTTP sessions might have a shorter timeout than file transfers or VoIP communications.

CBAC also includes capabilities for session thresholds and inspection limits. These features allow administrators to define the maximum number of sessions allowed per user or per protocol. This helps prevent misuse of resources or denial-of-service conditions caused by session flooding. If a user or an application tries to open more sessions than permitted, CBAC can deny the excess connections, protecting both the network and the device itself from overload. These thresholds are particularly useful in environments where specific users or devices might be compromised or misconfigured, leading to abnormal traffic behavior that could otherwise disrupt service for other users.

In addition to session tracking and dynamic rule creation, CBAC provides logging and alerting features. As it processes traffic, CBAC can log various events such as session creation, session deletion, protocol violations, and denied packets. These logs can be directed to local storage, remote syslog servers, or centralized security management systems for correlation and analysis. Logging helps administrators verify that policies are being enforced correctly, identify abnormal traffic patterns, and conduct forensic analysis following a security incident. The ability to generate real-time alerts based on CBAC events enhances the responsiveness of security teams and supports proactive threat mitigation.

From a configuration perspective, CBAC is implemented by first identifying the interface on which inspection should occur, typically an interface facing the external or untrusted side of the network. Inspection rules are then applied to traffic leaving the internal side toward the external interface. These rules define which protocols are subject to CBAC inspection, and optionally, the conditions under which sessions are created. Once configured, the firewall or router dynamically manages the inspection process based on the observed traffic. While the underlying inspection is automated, administrators retain full control over which traffic types are inspected, how long sessions remain active, and how session thresholds are enforced.

The effectiveness of CBAC lies in its ability to combine dynamic behavior with strict enforcement. It removes the need for static inbound access permissions while still enabling legitimate external responses to internal requests. It tracks traffic with intelligence, understands application behavior, and uses context to enforce rules. CBAC protects against a variety of threats, including spoofed packets, fragmented traffic, and unsolicited scans, all without sacrificing the accessibility required by legitimate users and applications. Its integration of inspection, logging, timeout enforcement, and session control makes it a comprehensive tool in any network administrator's arsenal. When used as part of a layered defense strategy, CBAC provides an additional level of depth that enhances overall network security and supports the reliable operation of mission-critical services in both enterprise and distributed environments.

Deep Packet Inspection with CBAC

Deep Packet Inspection, or DPI, when implemented with Context-Based Access Control (CBAC), introduces a more sophisticated layer of traffic analysis that enhances the security, reliability, and control of network communications. CBAC by itself provides stateful inspection, which is already a significant advancement over static filtering, but the addition of DPI allows CBAC to examine not just the headers of packets but also the payloads. This deeper level of inspection enables the system to recognize application-level behavior, enforce more granular security policies, detect protocol violations, and even identify malicious content embedded within seemingly legitimate traffic. When DPI is combined with CBAC, network devices are no longer limited to making decisions based solely on IP addresses and port numbers; they can now understand the context and content of the data being transmitted.

At the heart of deep packet inspection with CBAC is the ability to analyze packets beyond Layer 4 of the OSI model. While traditional firewalls and ACLs primarily inspect information at Layers 3 and 4, such as IP addresses, TCP/UDP port numbers, and simple session information, DPI delves into Layers 5 through 7, which include session, presentation, and application data. This capability allows CBAC to inspect entire data streams, reassemble fragmented packets, and interpret protocol-specific commands. For example, rather than merely identifying that traffic is HTTP-based, DPI enables CBAC to examine the HTTP request or response headers and body, identify the type of content being requested, and enforce policies based on that content.

This type of inspection becomes particularly useful when dealing with complex protocols that rely on dynamically assigned ports or contain multiple components within a single session. File Transfer Protocol (FTP) is a classic example. FTP uses separate control and data channels, and without DPI, a firewall would have to statically open a range of ports to allow file transfers to occur. With DPI-enhanced CBAC, the system can inspect the FTP control session, extract the necessary port information from the payload, and dynamically open only those ports required for the specific transfer. Once the transfer is complete, the temporary access is closed, reducing the exposure and risk associated with permanently open ports.

DPI also plays a critical role in identifying and mitigating evasion techniques used by attackers. Malicious actors often attempt to disguise their activities by tunneling dangerous payloads through legitimate protocols or by using non-standard ports to bypass traditional firewalls. For instance, malware might use HTTP or DNS to exfiltrate data or receive commands from a remote server, hoping that the firewall will allow the traffic simply because it appears to be web or domain traffic. DPI allows CBAC to go beyond surface-level inspection and analyze whether the content and structure of the protocol match its expected behavior. If anomalies are detected—such as encrypted payloads in a DNS request or command-and-control patterns within an HTTP stream—the traffic can be blocked or logged for further investigation.

Another key benefit of using DPI with CBAC is the ability to enforce application-aware policies. In today's networks, where multiple applications may share the same transport protocols, being able to distinguish between them becomes essential. For example, both web browsing and video streaming may use TCP port 443 over HTTPS, but they represent very different use cases and may require different levels of security and prioritization. With DPI, CBAC can differentiate between a user accessing an internal web application and someone watching high-definition video from a content provider. This distinction allows administrators to enforce bandwidth controls, prioritize critical business applications, and restrict non-essential usage without interfering with legitimate operations.

DPI-enhanced CBAC also strengthens defenses against advanced persistent threats and data loss. By examining payloads in real time, the system can detect sensitive information being transmitted in cleartext, unauthorized uploads of internal documents, or unusual patterns in outbound traffic that indicate data exfiltration attempts. CBAC can be configured to inspect specific types of content, such as email messages, file attachments, or database queries, and enforce rules based on keywords, file types, or data structures. This capability supports compliance efforts with regulations such as GDPR, HIPAA, or PCI-DSS by helping to prevent unauthorized transmission of personally identifiable information, healthcare records, or payment data.

Furthermore, DPI enables CBAC to handle encrypted traffic more effectively. While encryption is critical for privacy and security, it also poses a challenge for traditional inspection methods. DPI modules integrated with CBAC can decrypt SSL or TLS sessions at the firewall, inspect the content, and then re-encrypt the traffic before forwarding it. This process, known as SSL interception or SSL inspection, allows security policies to be enforced even on encrypted sessions. Administrators can use this feature to inspect HTTPS traffic for malicious content, enforce acceptable use policies, and block access to unauthorized services. At the same time, exceptions can be made for sensitive services, such as banking or medical websites, to protect user privacy while maintaining visibility where it is most needed.

The depth of inspection offered by DPI also improves logging and reporting capabilities. Rather than simply logging that a connection occurred on a specific port, CBAC with DPI can record what type of transaction occurred, which protocol elements were used, and whether any violations or anomalies were detected. These logs provide valuable insight for incident response, threat hunting, and auditing. When integrated with a Security Information and Event Management (SIEM) system, this rich contextual data can be correlated across multiple sources to detect multi-stage attacks or identify compromised endpoints within the network.

Implementing DPI with CBAC requires careful consideration of performance and resource consumption. Analyzing packet payloads in real time is computationally intensive and may introduce latency if not properly managed. High-performance firewalls and routers equipped with specialized hardware acceleration or dedicated inspection modules can mitigate this impact. Administrators must also define clear inspection policies to focus resources on high-risk or high-value traffic, rather than attempting to inspect every packet indiscriminately. Selective inspection based on zones, users, or application types helps maintain performance while maximizing security benefits.

From a configuration standpoint, administrators enable DPI by specifying which protocols should be inspected and which traffic flows are subject to deeper analysis. Rules can be applied based on the direction of traffic, the interface or zone involved, or the identity of users or devices. Advanced configurations may include thresholds for protocol anomalies, keyword detection, or file signature analysis. As threats evolve and applications become more sophisticated, these inspection rules must be regularly reviewed and updated to stay effective.

Ultimately, deep packet inspection with CBAC transforms a reactive security system into a proactive, intelligent layer of defense. By understanding not just where traffic is coming from and going to, but what it is actually doing, CBAC with DPI empowers network devices to make informed decisions about every session. It closes the gap between visibility and control, allowing security teams to detect threats earlier, respond faster, and enforce policies that align closely with both organizational needs and regulatory requirements. As networks continue to grow in complexity and threats become more evasive, the integration of DPI within CBAC will remain a critical element of advanced, adaptable, and resilient network security.

Protocol Inspection and Stateful Filtering

Protocol inspection and stateful filtering represent a significant advancement in network security, offering deeper visibility into communication flows and enabling more intelligent decisions about which traffic should be allowed or denied. Traditional packet filtering mechanisms, such as those found in basic access control lists, operate on a stateless basis. They evaluate individual packets in isolation, without context or awareness of the broader session to which the packets belong. This method, while simple and fast, has significant limitations. It cannot determine whether a packet is part of a legitimate connection, whether it is initiating a new session, or whether it matches a specific application behavior. Protocol inspection and stateful filtering address these limitations by keeping track of active connections and inspecting traffic at the protocol level, ensuring that only valid, expected communication is permitted.

Stateful filtering is the process by which a firewall or router tracks the state of active sessions as traffic flows through the device. When a connection is initiated, such as a TCP three-way handshake, the stateful firewall records key details about the session, including source and destination IP addresses, port numbers, and the protocol being used. As the session continues, the firewall monitors the ongoing exchange, keeping track of sequence numbers, flags, and connection states. This tracking allows the firewall to determine whether incoming packets are valid responses to existing sessions or unsolicited attempts to gain access. When a session is terminated, either gracefully or due to a timeout, the corresponding state table entry is removed. This lifecycle-based awareness provides a strong foundation for making access decisions that reflect the actual behavior of legitimate network communication.

Protocol inspection builds upon stateful filtering by examining the contents and structure of traffic according to the rules of the protocol in use. Rather than simply acknowledging that a session exists, protocol inspection involves analyzing how that session is behaving. For instance, in an FTP session, the protocol defines a specific sequence of commands and responses that must occur. A firewall with protocol inspection capabilities can monitor this sequence and determine whether the session is operating correctly or deviating in a way that might indicate an exploit attempt or misuse. This layer of analysis enables more precise enforcement and helps detect threats that may otherwise pass undetected through traditional filters.

One of the key benefits of protocol inspection is its ability to support dynamic protocol behavior. Many modern applications use dynamic port assignments, multiple channels, or embedded control data to establish secondary connections. These behaviors can be difficult or impossible to manage with static rules alone. For example, in a VoIP environment, protocols such as SIP and H.323 use control messages to set up media streams on dynamically selected ports. Without protocol inspection, administrators would have to open wide port ranges to support these communications, increasing the attack surface. With protocol inspection and stateful filtering, the firewall can examine the initial control messages, extract the port information, and temporarily open only those specific ports required for the media stream, closing them again once the session ends.

Another crucial advantage is the ability to detect and block protocol anomalies. Attackers often attempt to evade detection by manipulating protocol behavior, using malformed packets, or embedding malicious payloads in otherwise legitimate traffic. Stateful inspection with protocol awareness can identify these anomalies and take action accordingly. For example, an HTTP session that includes unexpected or out-of-order commands, overly long headers, or embedded executable content can be flagged or blocked. The firewall can maintain profiles of expected protocol behavior and reject any traffic that falls outside those norms. This proactive stance helps defend against a range of threats, including zero-day attacks, command injection, and session hijacking.

Protocol inspection also enhances the control over encrypted traffic. As more applications adopt SSL and TLS to secure their communications, the challenge for firewalls is maintaining visibility into encrypted sessions. Many modern stateful firewalls support SSL inspection, where the firewall acts as an intermediary between client and server, decrypting and inspecting traffic before re-encrypting it and passing it along. This enables deep inspection of protocols such as HTTPS, allowing organizations to enforce content filtering, block access to malicious sites, and detect data exfiltration attempts hidden within encrypted sessions. Combined with protocol inspection, SSL inspection ensures that security policies are applied consistently across all traffic, not just cleartext communications.

Session awareness, a hallmark of stateful filtering, also contributes to better resource management and performance optimization. By maintaining session state, the firewall can avoid re-evaluating each packet individually. It can quickly determine that a packet belongs to an existing, permitted session and forward it without additional processing. This efficiency reduces CPU load and latency, particularly in high-throughput environments. Moreover, administrators can configure session limits, timeouts, and idle thresholds to prevent resource exhaustion caused by too many open sessions or incomplete handshakes, which are often symptoms of denial-of-service attacks.

From a policy enforcement perspective, stateful and protocol-aware filtering allow for more nuanced and granular rules. Instead of creating static rules that allow all traffic on a given port, policies can be tied to specific applications, user identities, or behaviors. For example, a rule might allow web traffic only if it conforms to the expected structure of a legitimate HTTPS session, originates from a known subnet, and is initiated by an authenticated user. Protocol inspection can validate these conditions, and the stateful firewall can enforce them across the life of the session. This context-aware approach to rule enforcement supports compliance, reduces risk, and provides better alignment with business objectives.

In complex enterprise environments, the combination of stateful filtering and protocol inspection also simplifies troubleshooting and incident response. Logs generated by these systems provide detailed information about session initiation, duration, protocol behavior, and any violations that occur. This data is invaluable for diagnosing connectivity issues, investigating suspicious activity, or reconstructing the timeline of a security incident. Because the firewall understands the context of each session, it can provide more meaningful alerts and reduce the volume of false positives that often plague traditional detection systems.

Stateful filtering and protocol inspection together represent a comprehensive approach to modern network security. They allow organizations to maintain tight control over how applications communicate, ensure that only valid traffic is allowed, and detect threats at both the network and application layers. As threats grow more sophisticated and network environments become increasingly dynamic, the role of these technologies becomes even more essential. Their ability to combine awareness, adaptability, and intelligence positions them as core components of any defense-in-depth strategy, enabling organizations to build secure, resilient, and responsive networks that meet the challenges of today's digital landscape.

ChatGPT Plus

Session Awareness and Timeout Management

Session awareness and timeout management are central elements of modern network security and traffic control systems, particularly in stateful firewalls and advanced filtering mechanisms such as Context-Based Access Control. These features work together to provide security systems with the intelligence needed to manage ongoing communications based on the state of connections, rather than relying solely on static rules or isolated packet inspection. Session awareness allows a firewall or network device to track the status and lifecycle of each individual communication session, while timeout management ensures that sessions are closed automatically when they are no longer active. Together, these functions provide a dynamic and secure framework for managing the flow of traffic across network boundaries.

Session awareness begins when a new communication attempt is detected, such as the initiation of a TCP handshake or a UDP request. The network device recognizes this as the beginning of a session and records essential metadata about it. This metadata typically includes source and destination IP addresses, source and destination ports, protocol type, and connection state. Once this information is captured, it is stored in a session table maintained by the device. From that point forward, all subsequent packets associated with the same session are identified by referencing this table. This mechanism allows the system to permit return traffic without requiring separate inbound rules, as long as it matches an existing, validated session. In effect, session awareness reduces the administrative overhead of manually writing rules for every possible communication direction while also enhancing security by filtering traffic dynamically.

The tracking of session states is particularly valuable in TCP connections, which involve multiple stages such as connection establishment, data transfer, and session termination. The stateful device monitors the TCP flags and sequence numbers to ensure the connection is progressing as expected. If a packet arrives with flags or sequence numbers that are inconsistent with the expected state, the session can be terminated or the packet can be dropped, thereby protecting against malformed or spoofed traffic. This session-level monitoring also applies to connectionless protocols like UDP and ICMP, although in those cases, session tracking is based on timing and observed behavior rather than an explicit connection setup and teardown.

Timeout management plays a critical role in conserving system resources and enhancing security. Each tracked session has an associated timeout value, which determines how long the session remains active in the session table when no traffic is seen. Once the timeout period expires, the session entry is purged, and any further traffic from the same source must initiate a new session to be considered valid. Timeout values are protocol-specific and configurable. For example, a short timeout may be appropriate for DNS queries or ICMP messages, which are typically brief, while longer timeouts may be needed for protocols such as HTTPS or FTP, which involve longer-lived interactions. Carefully tuning these timeout values is important for both performance and security. If timeouts are too short, legitimate sessions may be dropped prematurely, causing users to experience connectivity issues. If timeouts are too long, stale or idle sessions may remain open unnecessarily, increasing the attack surface and consuming valuable system memory.

Session timeout values also serve as a safeguard against various forms of network abuse and resource exhaustion attacks. Attackers may attempt to flood a network device with large numbers of incomplete or idle sessions in order to deplete memory and processing power. By enforcing strict timeout policies, the system can automatically remove inactive or half-open sessions, thus limiting the window of opportunity for such attacks to succeed. In protocols like TCP, where an attacker may initiate a connection but never complete the handshake, the firewall can use a shorter timeout for half-open sessions, ensuring that resources are not tied up indefinitely.

Session awareness also enables more advanced features such as session-based logging, rate limiting, and connection quotas. When a device knows which sessions are active and who initiated them, it can generate more accurate and useful logs that capture the details of each connection. This information can include timestamps, volume of data transferred, duration of the session, and session termination conditions. These detailed logs are valuable for auditing, compliance reporting, troubleshooting, and forensic analysis. Furthermore, session awareness allows administrators to implement limits on the number of concurrent sessions per user, device, or subnet. This control helps prevent abuse by users who might otherwise consume excessive resources or by attackers attempting to establish a large number of sessions for scanning or exfiltration purposes.

In large networks or multi-tenant environments, timeout management can also be adapted to reflect different risk profiles or usage patterns. For example, public guest networks may have much shorter session timeouts compared to internal enterprise systems, ensuring that idle devices do not maintain persistent connections. Similarly, administrative or management traffic may warrant longer timeouts due to the nature of configuration sessions and system monitoring tools, which may be idle for extended periods before resuming activity. Implementing variable timeout policies tailored to each zone or type of traffic adds a layer of precision to access control and system optimization.

Session awareness also enhances interoperability and compatibility with other network functions. Quality of Service mechanisms can use session data to prioritize traffic by type or application, while intrusion detection systems can correlate session behavior with known attack patterns. In VPN environments, session tracking ensures that tunneled traffic is monitored with the same granularity as native traffic, preventing unauthorized access through the VPN channel. Likewise, session-based policies support application-layer firewalls and deep packet inspection engines by providing context to the content being analyzed. When combined with user identity, session information can also facilitate identity-aware firewalls, which enforce policies based not only on IP or port but on who is initiating the session and what role they have in the organization.

Ultimately, the integration of session awareness and timeout management results in a more responsive and intelligent security infrastructure. Rather than relying on a rigid set of rules, the system adapts dynamically to the behavior of traffic in real time. This adaptability reduces the complexity of security configurations while increasing their effectiveness. Network administrators gain better control over how connections are established, maintained, and terminated, allowing them to fine-tune performance, protect resources, and respond to emerging threats with speed and precision. As networks become more dynamic and as the boundary between trusted and untrusted environments continues to blur, session awareness and timeout management will remain essential tools in ensuring the secure and efficient operation of modern digital ecosystems.

Creating CBAC Inspection Rules

Creating Context-Based Access Control inspection rules is a critical step in implementing dynamic, stateful traffic filtering in a secure network environment. These rules define which protocols should be inspected, on which interfaces the inspection should take place, and under what conditions traffic is permitted or denied. Unlike traditional access control lists that statically allow or block traffic based on simple criteria, CBAC inspection rules analyze the behavior of connections over time. This stateful inspection allows for temporary, dynamic openings in the firewall that close automatically when sessions end, significantly reducing the risk of unauthorized access or misuse. The process of creating CBAC rules must be carried out with a clear understanding of network flows, application behavior, and organizational security policies to ensure effectiveness without disrupting legitimate operations.

The process begins by identifying the traffic that needs to be inspected. CBAC is protocol-aware, which means it supports a range of common services such as HTTP, HTTPS, FTP, SMTP, DNS, SIP, and others. Administrators must determine which protocols are used by internal clients to access external resources and define inspection rules accordingly. For example, if users access external websites, then HTTP and HTTPS must be included in the inspection policy. Similarly, if file transfers are required, FTP inspection should be enabled. The goal is to inspect only necessary protocols to minimize processing overhead while maximizing security benefits. It is important to avoid overly broad inspection rules, as they can introduce latency and consume unnecessary system resources.

Once the required protocols have been selected, the next step is defining the direction of inspection. CBAC is typically configured to inspect outbound traffic on an internal interface, such as the one facing the LAN. When traffic that matches the defined protocol and direction is detected, CBAC inspects the session and dynamically creates temporary access rules on the external interface to allow return traffic. This process eliminates the need for explicit inbound rules, which would otherwise remain open indefinitely and pose a security risk. By focusing inspection on outbound traffic, CBAC leverages the principle of initiating trust: only traffic that originates from within the trusted network and establishes a valid session is allowed to receive responses from the untrusted side.

To implement inspection rules, administrators must use commands to define an inspection policy and apply it to the desired interface. In Cisco environments, this involves creating a named inspection rule using the ip inspect name command followed by the protocol to be inspected. For example, ip inspect name OUTBOUND_TRAFFIC http would define an inspection rule for HTTP traffic under the label OUTBOUND_TRAFFIC. Multiple protocols can be added under the same policy name, building a group of services to be inspected together. After defining the inspection rule, it is applied to the relevant interface using the ip inspect OUTBOUND_TRAFFIC out command. This tells the router to inspect outbound traffic on that interface using the specified rule set.

Timeout values are another important aspect of CBAC inspection rules. Each protocol may require different idle timeout settings to reflect typical usage patterns. For example, HTTP sessions might be short-lived and benefit from a shorter timeout, while protocols such as SSH or Telnet, which often involve longer interactive sessions, might require extended timeouts to avoid premature termination. CBAC allows the administrator to set custom timeout values per protocol using the ip inspect <protocol> timeout command. These settings should be tuned based on actual traffic behavior, balancing the need for resource conservation with the user experience. Timely session expiration also helps mitigate the risk of attackers exploiting abandoned or idle sessions.

CBAC inspection rules can also include session thresholds to prevent denial-of-service attacks or misconfigured applications from overwhelming the network device. Administrators can limit the number of concurrent sessions per protocol or per user. For example, if an application is known to open multiple simultaneous connections, but only a few are necessary for normal operation, a session limit can be enforced to detect and block excessive connection attempts. This feature protects the router from resource exhaustion and helps maintain service availability during heavy usage or attack scenarios. Session audit logs can further assist in identifying problematic hosts or applications that violate normal usage patterns.

In addition to traffic inspection and stateful session tracking, CBAC rules also enable advanced features like alerting and logging. Administrators can configure logging of session creation, deletion, and violations using the ip inspect log command. This provides valuable insight into how CBAC rules are functioning, which protocols are being used, and whether any suspicious or malformed traffic is being blocked. Logs can be directed to a syslog server or reviewed locally for analysis. Effective logging not only supports security operations but also aids in troubleshooting, policy tuning, and compliance reporting. Ensuring that inspection rules include appropriate logging directives enhances visibility and control without adding complexity to the rule set.

Creating CBAC inspection rules also involves understanding how different protocols interact and how multi-channel communications should be handled. Certain protocols, such as FTP or SIP, require dynamic handling of secondary connections. CBAC is capable of interpreting these control messages and opening related data channels on the fly. Inspection rules should be configured to support these protocols explicitly so that their multi-port behavior is properly handled. Without CBAC's intelligent handling, administrators would have to open large port ranges permanently, introducing security risks. By leveraging CBAC's dynamic rule generation, administrators can ensure that only necessary ports are opened and only for the duration of the session.

When designing CBAC inspection rules, it is essential to test them in a staging environment before deployment to production. Misconfigured rules can lead to blocked traffic, application failures, or unexpected behavior. Staged testing allows for validation of expected flows, monitoring of session creation and teardown, and fine-tuning of timeout or threshold parameters. Once deployed, ongoing monitoring is necessary to ensure that inspection rules continue to align with evolving network needs. As new applications are added or services change, CBAC rules should be reviewed and updated accordingly. Rule sets should not remain static; they must evolve with the network to remain effective and efficient.

In a comprehensive security architecture, CBAC inspection rules play a foundational role in enforcing secure and controlled access across network boundaries. They bring context to traffic evaluation, supporting both operational continuity and strong defense against unauthorized access. By creating well-defined, protocol-specific inspection policies and applying them thoughtfully to the right interfaces, administrators empower the network to make intelligent decisions about what traffic should be allowed and under what conditions. Through careful configuration, continuous monitoring, and thoughtful policy design, CBAC inspection rules transform traditional filtering into a dynamic and responsive security control that adapts to real-time conditions and contributes meaningfully to a robust defense-in-depth strategy.

Monitoring CBAC Sessions

Monitoring CBAC sessions is an essential task in maintaining visibility, performance, and security in a network that relies on Context-Based Access Control. Because CBAC dynamically inspects and manages traffic flows based on session behavior, administrators must have a clear understanding of how these sessions are created, maintained, and terminated. Visibility into these sessions allows for better decision-making when troubleshooting, optimizing policy configurations, or responding to unusual activity. Without proper monitoring, it becomes difficult to validate that inspection policies are working as intended, and even harder to detect performance bottlenecks or identify emerging threats in real time. Monitoring ensures that the dynamic nature of CBAC does not obscure the flow of information through the network but instead provides a structured, observable framework that can be used to analyze and fine-tune access control strategies.

When CBAC is enabled on a router or firewall, it begins to track sessions by building a state table. This state table contains detailed information about every session that is allowed through the network, including the source and destination IP addresses, port numbers, protocol types, and the direction of traffic flow. Additionally, the table captures the duration of each session and whether the session is active, idle, or terminated. Administrators can access this information through CLI commands such as show ip inspect sessions, which provides a real-time snapshot of all currently inspected sessions. This command helps administrators observe which protocols are in use, how many concurrent sessions exist, and where traffic is flowing across network boundaries.

Regular monitoring of this session table is critical for capacity planning and resource management. Each active session consumes memory and processing resources on the device. In environments with high volumes of traffic or many concurrent users, the number of sessions can grow quickly. If left unchecked, this growth can lead to performance degradation or even failure of the inspection engine due to exhausted resources. By monitoring session counts over time, administrators can establish baseline activity levels and recognize deviations from normal patterns. If a sudden spike in session activity occurs, it may indicate an event such as a denial-of-service attack or misconfigured application attempting to open too many simultaneous connections.

CBAC session monitoring is also a vital tool in the troubleshooting process. When users report connectivity problems, session tracking can help identify whether traffic is being correctly inspected and whether dynamic access rules are being created as expected. For example, if an internal user cannot access an external service, administrators can check the session table to see if the outbound request was inspected and whether a corresponding return path has been dynamically permitted. If no session entry is found, this may suggest that the inspection rule is not applied correctly or that the traffic type is not covered by the policy. If the session exists but is stuck in an idle or half-open state, this could indicate network delays or asymmetric routing issues that must be resolved.

In addition to the session table, CBAC provides a set of counters and statistics that track the performance and effectiveness of inspection policies. These counters record the number of sessions created, the number terminated due to timeout, the number dropped due to exceeding thresholds, and any protocol violations detected during inspection. These metrics are accessible via the show ip inspect statistics command, which aggregates the data for each protocol and inspection rule. Reviewing these statistics regularly helps administrators understand which services are being used, how often inspections are triggered, and whether certain policies are generating errors or consuming excessive resources. This insight is crucial for optimizing inspection rules and maintaining a healthy balance between security and performance.

Monitoring also extends to tracking session timeouts and idle durations. CBAC maintains timeout values for each protocol, defining how long a session may remain open without activity. By analyzing the frequency of timeout expirations, administrators can determine whether the configured timeout values are appropriate for the actual behavior of network applications. If sessions are timing out too frequently, it may result in poor user experience or interrupted services. Conversely, if sessions remain open for too long without activity, it increases the risk of unauthorized access or resource exhaustion. Adjusting timeout values based on monitoring data allows the inspection system to remain both responsive and secure.

Another important aspect of monitoring CBAC sessions involves detecting abnormal behavior or suspicious patterns. For instance, if an internal host begins opening hundreds of outbound sessions in a short period of time, this might indicate the presence of malware or an infected device participating in a botnet. By monitoring session initiation rates, administrators can quickly identify such anomalies and take corrective action, such as isolating the affected device or tightening inspection thresholds. Likewise, monitoring repeated failed session initiations or protocol violations can help uncover misconfigured devices or malicious actors probing the network for weaknesses.

Integrating CBAC session monitoring with broader network management systems enhances visibility and supports centralized oversight. Session data and inspection statistics can be exported to external monitoring platforms using syslog or SNMP, allowing administrators to correlate session behavior with other network events. This integration supports proactive incident response and helps build a comprehensive picture of network activity. By combining CBAC session monitoring with logs, flow data, and endpoint telemetry, security teams gain the situational awareness needed to detect and contain threats before they escalate into major incidents.

In more advanced environments, automated tools can be used to analyze CBAC session data in real time. These tools apply machine learning or pattern recognition techniques to detect deviations from normal behavior and alert administrators to potential issues. For example, an automated system might recognize that a particular service is suddenly being accessed far more frequently than usual and flag it for review. These tools can also assist in policy tuning by identifying inspection rules that are rarely triggered or session types that consistently cause errors. As networks continue to evolve and threats become more sophisticated, automated analysis of session data will play a growing role in maintaining secure and efficient operations.

Ultimately, the ability to monitor CBAC sessions is one of the key reasons why CBAC is considered a powerful and intelligent form of access control. It transforms the firewall from a static barrier into a dynamic security platform that not only makes decisions based on session context but also provides the visibility necessary to validate those decisions. Monitoring enables administrators to understand how their inspection policies function in real environments, supports rapid diagnosis of connectivity issues, and provides a critical source of data for continuous improvement. In a world where visibility is often the first line of defense, effective CBAC session monitoring is not optional—it is an operational necessity for any network that relies on stateful inspection to manage and secure its traffic.

Troubleshooting CBAC Configurations

Troubleshooting CBAC configurations is a vital skill for network administrators responsible for ensuring secure and reliable traffic inspection and filtering within enterprise networks. Context-Based Access Control offers dynamic, stateful inspection capabilities, but its flexibility and complexity also introduce potential for misconfiguration. When CBAC is not functioning as expected, users may experience blocked applications, intermittent connectivity, or complete communication failures. These issues can arise from several factors, including incorrect inspection rule definitions, misapplied policies on interfaces, protocol-specific behavior, timeout mismatches, or conflicts with other access control mechanisms such as ACLs. Diagnosing and resolving these problems requires a methodical approach, a clear understanding of how CBAC operates, and familiarity with the tools available for observation and verification.

One of the first steps in troubleshooting a CBAC issue is to determine whether the inspection rules are correctly defined and applied. CBAC rules are created using the ip inspect name command followed by a policy name and protocol, and they must be applied to the correct interface and direction using the ip inspect command. A common mistake is applying the inspection rule to the wrong interface or in the incorrect direction. For example, applying an outbound inspection rule on an external-facing interface will prevent the system from dynamically allowing return traffic, because CBAC only inspects traffic in the direction of the initial session initiation. This means that inspection rules should typically be applied to the internal interface in the outbound direction. Verifying interface assignments and ensuring that inspection rules are present where traffic originates is an essential early step.

Once the basic configuration is verified, the administrator should inspect active CBAC sessions using the show ip inspect sessions command. This command reveals whether traffic is actually being inspected and whether session entries are being created dynamically. If no sessions appear for traffic that should be inspected, it may indicate that the rule is not matching the traffic, perhaps due to a mismatch in protocol or incorrect identification of the traffic flow. For instance, if users are accessing HTTPS services but the inspection rule only includes HTTP, no sessions will be created, and return traffic will be denied. Ensuring the correct protocols are specified in the inspection rule is critical. Administrators must also be aware of application behaviors that span multiple ports or use non-standard ports, as CBAC relies on expected protocol structures unless configured otherwise.

Timeout settings can also cause inspection-related issues. If sessions are timing out too quickly, legitimate traffic may be dropped, leading to intermittent failures or slow application performance. Each protocol inspected by CBAC can be assigned a specific idle timeout value, and if this value is too short for the application in question, the session may be removed prematurely. Conversely, long timeout values may lead to stale sessions that consume resources unnecessarily or allow unintended access. Reviewing timeout configurations with the show ip inspect config or show running-config commands and comparing them to observed session durations can help administrators adjust values for better reliability. Inconsistent session behavior often traces back to a mismatch between real-world traffic patterns and configured timeout policies.

Another potential source of trouble is the interaction between CBAC and traditional access control lists. If an inbound ACL is applied to an external interface and it does not allow return traffic for CBAC-inspected sessions, the traffic will be dropped even though the inspection system attempted to permit it dynamically. This is because ACLs are processed before CBAC session matches in some platform-specific implementations. To avoid this conflict, ACLs must be configured to allow traffic that CBAC is expected to permit dynamically. One common best practice is to keep ACLs minimal and rely on CBAC to manage session-based access where applicable. In cases where ACLs and CBAC must coexist, their configurations must be carefully coordinated to avoid unintentional blocks.

Logging can provide valuable clues when troubleshooting CBAC. If logging is enabled for inspection rules, using the ip inspect log drop-pkt command, dropped packets due to inspection failures will be recorded and can be reviewed through syslog or the router's internal buffer. These logs indicate why a packet was denied, such as a timeout expiration, a violation of expected protocol behavior, or an attempt to open a connection in the reverse direction. Reviewing these logs alongside session information can quickly narrow down the cause of access issues. For persistent problems, enabling full logging temporarily during testing phases can provide comprehensive data to pinpoint misbehavior.

Protocol-specific anomalies are another source of CBAC issues. Some protocols, such as FTP or SIP, use dynamic port negotiation or secondary sessions, and CBAC must interpret control messages correctly to allow associated data flows. If CBAC is not properly inspecting these control sessions, the data sessions will be blocked. For instance, passive FTP may not work as expected unless the inspection engine understands the control messages and opens the negotiated data ports dynamically. When these types of applications fail, administrators should confirm that the corresponding protocols are explicitly listed in the inspection rules and that no intermediate devices are interfering with protocol signaling.

In multi-zone or complex topologies, asymmetric routing can interfere with CBAC operation. If a connection is initiated through one path and the return traffic follows a different route that bypasses the inspection-enabled interface, the CBAC session will not be recognized, and the return traffic will be dropped. Ensuring symmetric routing through policy-based routing or adjusting network paths may be necessary to guarantee that both directions of traffic pass through the same CBAC inspection point. This is especially important in environments with multiple WAN links or redundant paths.

Additionally, CBAC's interaction with NAT can lead to unexpected behavior if the session table does not correctly correlate translated addresses with the original session. When NAT is performed before CBAC inspection, the inspection engine may fail to match return traffic to the correct session. Administrators should verify the order of operations on their device and ensure that NAT configurations do not disrupt inspection logic. This often involves confirming that CBAC inspects the traffic after NAT translation has taken place or using NAT mappings that preserve essential session details.

Troubleshooting CBAC configurations requires a combination of observation, verification, and adjustment. Each component—interface direction, inspection rules, protocol coverage, timeout settings, ACL interactions, routing paths, and NAT—plays a role in the correct functioning of CBAC. Any misstep can lead to traffic being unnecessarily blocked or allowed, undermining the balance of security and accessibility that CBAC is designed to provide. By following a systematic process of checking configurations, examining live session data, interpreting logs, and understanding application behavior, administrators can resolve issues effectively and restore reliable access while maintaining the high level of security CBAC is meant to deliver.

Performance Tuning with CBAC

Performance tuning with Context-Based Access Control is an essential aspect of maintaining an efficient and responsive network while upholding a high standard of security. CBAC introduces a dynamic layer of stateful inspection that monitors session behavior and enforces protocol rules, which offers robust protection but also introduces additional processing demands on the firewall or router. As inspection rules increase in complexity and as traffic volumes grow, the performance of the device can be affected if configurations are not optimized. Administrators must carefully tune CBAC settings to ensure that the system can handle current and anticipated loads without becoming a bottleneck or introducing latency that disrupts end-user experience or business-critical applications.

The first step in performance tuning is understanding the hardware capabilities of the device running CBAC. Each platform has limitations in terms of processing power, memory, and throughput. Stateful inspection consumes CPU cycles and memory to track each active session and evaluate traffic against inspection rules. Devices with limited resources may begin to exhibit slowdowns as session counts increase or as more protocols are added to the inspection list. It is essential to monitor resource utilization during peak traffic periods and correlate performance drops with CBAC activity. If high CPU utilization coincides with a large number of concurrent sessions, this is an indicator that the inspection workload needs to be optimized.

One effective method of performance optimization is the careful selection of protocols for inspection. Not all traffic needs to be inspected by CBAC. Administrators should identify which applications and services require stateful inspection for security purposes and which can be managed through static ACLs or left uninspected due to low risk. For example, internal-only services or encrypted tunnels that already provide end-to-end security may not benefit from inspection. By limiting CBAC to essential protocols such as HTTP, HTTPS, FTP, DNS, and mail-related traffic, administrators can reduce the inspection burden while still protecting the majority of vulnerable services. Removing unnecessary protocols from the inspection list also reduces the size of the session table and lowers the chances of session tracking errors.

Adjusting session timeouts is another critical tuning measure. Every protocol tracked by CBAC has an associated timeout value that determines how long an idle session remains in the session table. If these values are set too high, stale sessions may linger and consume memory unnecessarily. On the other hand, if timeouts are too short, active sessions may be prematurely dropped, leading to failed transactions and poor application performance. Tuning these values involves finding a balance based on observed traffic patterns. Administrators should monitor session durations and adjust timeouts to reflect real-world usage, ensuring that active sessions are maintained while idle sessions are cleaned up promptly. Timeouts for short-lived protocols such as DNS can often be reduced, while interactive sessions like SSH may need longer durations.

In environments with high session turnover, session limits per protocol or per interface can help prevent resource exhaustion. CBAC allows administrators to define thresholds that limit the number of concurrent sessions for specific protocols or users. These limits can prevent individual hosts or misbehaving applications from overwhelming the inspection engine with excessive connections. If a system attempts to exceed the allowed threshold, additional session requests can be dropped or logged, protecting the network from degradation. Properly configured thresholds protect both the device and the broader network from misuse or attack without impacting legitimate traffic when properly sized.

Another important aspect of tuning involves the granularity of inspection rules. Overly broad rules that apply to large ranges of ports or IP addresses can force CBAC to examine far more traffic than necessary. Conversely, overly granular rules can increase the size and complexity of the inspection table and slow down rule matching. Administrators must design inspection policies that are specific enough to enforce security policies without being so detailed that they impair performance. This often means grouping services logically, inspecting common application groups together, and avoiding wildcard configurations that encompass unnecessary or irrelevant traffic.

Logging configuration also has a direct impact on performance. While logging is essential for monitoring, diagnostics, and compliance, excessive or verbose logging can consume processing resources and generate large volumes of data. CBAC allows for selective logging of dropped packets, session creation, and protocol violations. To tune performance, administrators can limit logging to high-priority events or apply sampling strategies to reduce the volume of log entries.

Additionally, logs should be exported to external syslog servers or security information and event management systems, rather than being stored locally on the device, to prevent storage constraints from affecting inspection operations.

In some implementations, CBAC can be augmented with hardware acceleration or offloading capabilities. High-end routers and firewalls may include dedicated processors or modules specifically designed for inspection tasks. Where available, enabling these features can offload the most demanding aspects of CBAC and free the main CPU for other tasks. This is particularly useful in high-throughput environments where inspection must be performed at line rate. Administrators should ensure that CBAC is configured to take advantage of available hardware resources and that firmware or software updates are applied to maintain optimal compatibility and performance.

Regular review of inspection statistics is also an essential component of performance tuning. Commands such as show ip inspect statistics provide valuable insight into session counts, per-protocol activity, and packet inspection rates. These statistics can be used to identify trends, detect unusual usage patterns, and determine which protocols or sessions are consuming the most resources. By correlating this data with performance metrics such as CPU load and memory usage, administrators can make informed decisions about which rules need adjustment or which traffic patterns require further analysis.

In complex networks, CBAC may be used in conjunction with other features such as NAT, VPN tunnels, or application-layer gateways. Each of these can introduce additional overhead or affect inspection logic. Performance tuning must take into account the interplay between these features and CBAC. For instance, NAT configurations should be carefully coordinated with inspection rules to ensure that session tracking is accurate and efficient. In VPN environments, administrators should evaluate whether encrypted traffic needs to be decrypted before inspection and, if so, ensure that resources are sufficient to handle the combined workload of decryption and inspection.

Ultimately, performance tuning with CBAC is not a one-time task but an ongoing process that must evolve with changes in network traffic, user behavior, and application requirements. As new services are introduced or existing ones are modified, inspection policies must be reviewed to ensure they remain efficient and effective. By adopting a proactive approach that includes monitoring, analysis, and periodic adjustment, administrators can maintain a balance between strong security enforcement and high network performance. This balance is critical to supporting business operations while defending against a constantly changing threat landscape. CBAC offers powerful capabilities, but only when it is properly tuned to the needs and constraints of the environment in which it operates.

ACL Optimization Strategies

Access Control Lists play a foundational role in controlling traffic flow, enforcing security policies, and segmenting network resources. However, as networks grow in size and complexity, the number of ACL entries can increase significantly, leading to potential performance degradation and increased management difficulty. Optimization strategies are essential to maintain the efficiency, clarity, and responsiveness of ACL implementations. Properly optimized ACLs not only improve processing performance on routers and firewalls but also enhance security by reducing the likelihood of misconfiguration and unnecessary rule overlap. Effective optimization begins with a thorough understanding of the ACL structure, the order in which rules are processed, and the behavior of the traffic being filtered.

One of the most important aspects of ACL optimization is rule ordering. ACLs are processed sequentially from top to bottom, and the first matching rule dictates the action taken. This means that frequently matched rules should be placed near the top of the ACL to minimize processing time. If the most-used rules are buried deep within a long list, the device must evaluate every preceding entry before arriving at the correct match, consuming CPU resources with every packet. Administrators should analyze traffic patterns using flow analysis tools or logs to determine which rules are most commonly matched. Once identified, these rules should be prioritized and reordered to improve processing efficiency. The ability to reorder ACLs based on usage statistics is a critical practice for performance tuning.

Another essential optimization strategy is rule consolidation. In many cases, separate ACL entries can be combined into a single entry using subnet summarization or range specifications. For example, multiple permit statements for contiguous IP addresses or ports can often be collapsed into one using a wildcard mask or range. This reduces the total number of lines in the ACL, simplifies readability, and speeds up processing. Careful subnet planning also supports this approach, allowing IP addresses to be grouped logically and consistently across the network. When designing ACLs, administrators should look for opportunities to use network prefixes, port ranges, or protocol groupings that cover multiple requirements with a single rule.

Minimizing redundancy is another key principle in ACL optimization. Over time, as new rules are added to accommodate evolving business requirements or troubleshooting activities, ACLs can become cluttered with duplicate or conflicting entries. These redundant rules not only waste processing time but can also create confusion during audits or changes. Regularly reviewing ACLs to identify and remove duplicate entries or rules that are overridden by earlier matches is essential. Tools that support ACL analysis can assist in identifying redundancies, shadowed rules, or unreachable entries. Keeping ACLs lean and free of unnecessary complexity enhances both performance and manageability.

Using named ACLs instead of numbered ones is a best practice that contributes indirectly to optimization by improving manageability. Named ACLs are easier to reference, modify, and document. While they do not offer a performance benefit in themselves, they make it easier for administrators to understand the purpose of each ACL and to implement structured naming conventions that reflect their function. A well-organized naming scheme supports faster identification and editing of rules, especially in environments where multiple ACLs are applied across different interfaces or devices. This clarity becomes particularly valuable when implementing optimization strategies that require rule movement, deletion, or reordering.

Proper placement of ACLs in the network topology also affects optimization. In general, standard ACLs should be placed as close as possible to the destination, since they filter only by source address and can unintentionally block broader ranges of traffic if placed too close to the source. Extended ACLs, on the other hand, should be placed close to the source to prevent unwanted traffic from traversing the network unnecessarily. Applying this principle consistently not only improves security but also reduces bandwidth consumption and processing overhead on intermediate devices. By filtering traffic as early as appropriate in the path, ACLs can minimize the burden on network links and improve end-to-end efficiency.

Logging within ACLs is a useful feature for auditing and troubleshooting, but excessive logging can have a negative impact on performance. Logging causes the device to generate additional messages for every packet that matches a rule with the log keyword, consuming processing resources and potentially overwhelming log servers or buffers. For optimization purposes, logging should be applied selectively to rules where visibility is critical, such as deny statements at the end of an ACL or rules that protect sensitive services. Limiting the number of log-generating rules and controlling the volume of log messages helps maintain system stability while still capturing valuable data.

Scalability is another important consideration in ACL optimization, especially in dynamic or large-scale environments. Static ACLs may become difficult to manage as the number of users, services, or subnets increases. Integrating ACLs with dynamic features such as object groups or identity-based access control can streamline management and reduce duplication. Object groups allow multiple IP addresses, networks, or services to be referenced in a single rule, dramatically reducing the size of ACLs while maintaining precision. This abstraction layer simplifies changes and supports more scalable policy definitions, particularly in enterprise networks with frequent changes.

Automation tools can further enhance optimization by generating and managing ACLs based on templates, policies, or real-time network conditions. These tools can evaluate traffic flows, suggest ACL modifications, and automatically deploy updated configurations across multiple devices. By automating routine ACL tasks and optimization checks, organizations can reduce human error and accelerate response times to emerging security needs. Integrating ACL optimization into automated configuration management pipelines ensures that rules remain efficient and relevant over time, rather than becoming outdated or overly permissive.

ACL optimization is not only a technical process but also a policy-driven one. It requires coordination with security teams, application owners, and operational stakeholders to ensure that rule changes align with organizational needs. Regular reviews, audits, and validations must be conducted to confirm that optimized ACLs continue to meet their intended objectives. Incorporating feedback loops where rule effectiveness and performance are continuously evaluated fosters a culture of continuous improvement. This approach not only enhances security posture but also ensures that network performance and user experience are not sacrificed in pursuit of access control.

In modern networks where performance, security, and agility are all paramount, ACL optimization is a vital practice that directly contributes to operational success. By reducing rule count, improving processing order, eliminating redundancy, and embracing automation, organizations can maintain high levels of control while avoiding the inefficiencies and complexities that often plague large-scale ACL deployments. Optimization ensures that ACLs remain an asset rather than a liability, delivering both protection and performance in a balanced and sustainable manner.

Security Policy Enforcement Techniques

Security policy enforcement techniques form the backbone of any effective cybersecurity framework, ensuring that defined rules and controls are applied consistently across the network infrastructure. These techniques transform high-level policy statements, such as those defining access permissions or data protection requirements, into actionable technical configurations that are enforced by network devices, firewalls, authentication systems, and endpoint protections. A security policy on its own is a set of intentions, but enforcement techniques ensure that these intentions are realized in the form of tangible access control, traffic filtering, user validation, and behavior monitoring. In modern network environments, where devices, users, and applications are constantly changing, robust and adaptable enforcement techniques are necessary to maintain control and limit exposure to threats.

One of the foundational techniques in policy enforcement is the application of access control lists on routers, switches, and firewalls. ACLs are used to filter traffic based on defined parameters such as source and destination IP addresses, protocol types, port numbers, and even time-based conditions. These lists are interpreted in a strict sequence, matching packets against each rule until a match is found, at which point the specified action, such as permit or deny, is executed. The enforcement of these rules directly reflects the organization's security posture, allowing only sanctioned communications while blocking unauthorized or unnecessary connections. Effective use of ACLs requires not only technical knowledge of the network topology and traffic patterns but also a clear understanding of the organization's access control policy objectives.

Context-based enforcement techniques, such as those provided by stateful firewalls and systems like CBAC, enhance traditional ACLs by considering the context of communication sessions. Stateful firewalls track the initiation and progression of connections, allowing return traffic for established sessions without the need for separate inbound rules. This approach ensures that policies are enforced based on session legitimacy, not just static packet attributes. By monitoring the state of each connection, these systems can enforce policy in a more intelligent and efficient manner. Context-aware systems can detect and block traffic that deviates from expected protocol behavior, offering a dynamic method of enforcement that adapts to the nature of the traffic flow.

Another critical enforcement technique is identity-based access control, which ties policy enforcement to user or device identity rather than just IP addresses or network segments. This method enables more granular policy application, allowing different users on the same subnet to receive different levels of access based on their roles, credentials, or device posture. Technologies like 802.1X authentication, network access control platforms, and identity-aware firewalls enable this approach by integrating with directory services such as Active Directory or LDAP. These systems can enforce policies at the point of network access, allowing or denying connections based on a combination of identity attributes and policy definitions. This technique is particularly useful in environments with mobile users, guest access, or bring-your-own-device policies.

Zone-based enforcement, using concepts such as security zones and trust levels, provides another layer of structured control. Network segments are grouped into logical zones based on function and sensitivity, such as internal user zones, data center zones, DMZs, and external interfaces. Policy is then applied to regulate traffic between these zones, often with different rules depending on the direction of traffic and the trust relationship between zones. For example, traffic from a user zone to a data zone may be tightly restricted and subject to inspection, while return traffic is permitted only within the scope of approved sessions. This method allows for scalable policy enforcement that aligns with architectural boundaries and reduces the risk of lateral movement by attackers.

Policy enforcement at the application layer is another increasingly vital technique, especially in environments that rely heavily on web applications and cloud services. Application-layer firewalls, proxies, and secure web gateways inspect traffic beyond the transport headers, analyzing the actual content and behavior of applications. Policies can be enforced based on application signatures, URL categories, file types, and content scanning. For example, a policy may prevent users from uploading files to external file-sharing services or from accessing websites categorized as malicious or inappropriate. Enforcement at this layer provides the visibility and control needed to manage risks that are invisible at the network layer, such as data exfiltration through legitimate-looking HTTPS connections.

Encryption-based enforcement, including the use of SSL/TLS inspection and VPN technologies, ensures that policy enforcement can occur even within secure tunnels. Encrypted traffic poses a challenge for traditional inspection methods, as the content is obscured. SSL inspection capabilities allow security appliances to decrypt, inspect, and re-encrypt traffic to apply security policies effectively. Likewise, VPNs enforce encryption and authentication policies, ensuring that only trusted users and devices can connect to internal resources. This technique extends the reach of enforcement policies into remote access scenarios and protects data in transit against eavesdropping or tampering.

Another technique central to modern enforcement is behavioral analysis and anomaly detection. Instead of relying solely on predefined rules, systems use machine learning algorithms or heuristic models to identify deviations from normal behavior that may indicate policy violations. Network behavior analysis tools can detect unusual login patterns, data transfer spikes, or unauthorized access attempts and trigger automated responses or alerts. While not a replacement for traditional enforcement methods, behavioral enforcement enhances detection capabilities and provides a dynamic layer of response that can adapt to evolving threats.

Time-based enforcement allows administrators to apply policies that vary depending on the time of day or day of the week. This is particularly useful in environments where access requirements change based on work schedules, maintenance windows, or business hours. For example, administrative access to sensitive systems might only be permitted during certain hours, or guest access might be disabled after office hours. This technique helps reduce the window of exposure and aligns access with operational needs, enhancing both security and compliance.

Data loss prevention techniques are also a form of enforcement that focuses on the control of sensitive information. These techniques include scanning content for predefined patterns such as credit card numbers, personal identifiers, or proprietary data before allowing it to leave the network. Enforcement can occur at the endpoint, at the perimeter, or within cloud environments, and actions may include blocking, alerting, or encrypting sensitive data. When integrated with broader security policies, DLP enforcement ensures that information handling practices align with organizational standards and legal obligations.

Security policy enforcement techniques are the mechanisms by which theoretical policy is translated into operational control. Each technique must be selected and implemented based on the nature of the environment, the risk posture of the organization, and the types of threats most likely to be encountered. Proper enforcement ensures consistency, visibility, and accountability, making it possible to detect and respond to violations, support compliance efforts, and maintain trust in the integrity of the network. As networks become more dynamic and complex, the ability to enforce policies in real time, across diverse environments, and with minimal disruption becomes not only a best practice but a fundamental requirement for maintaining security.

Hierarchical Firewall Designs

Hierarchical firewall designs represent an advanced approach to structuring security controls within a network architecture, focusing on layered and logically distributed protection rather than relying on a single, monolithic firewall implementation. In this model, multiple firewalls are strategically deployed at different points within the infrastructure, each responsible for enforcing security at a specific layer or segment of the network. This distribution of responsibilities enhances both security and scalability by ensuring that access controls and inspection policies are aligned with the function and sensitivity of each network zone. A hierarchical design is especially effective in large-scale enterprise environments, data centers, multi-tenant cloud architectures, and networks that support a wide range of services and user roles. It allows for the creation of trust boundaries and the implementation of tailored security controls, reducing the overall attack surface and enabling more precise traffic filtering.

At the core of a hierarchical firewall design is the concept of segmentation. Rather than funneling all traffic through a single firewall, the network is divided into multiple zones, each protected by one or more dedicated firewalls. The outermost layer typically includes a perimeter firewall, which serves as the first line of defense between the internal network and external threats. This firewall enforces coarse-grained policies such as allowing or blocking entire protocols, IP ranges, or geographical regions. It focuses primarily on preventing unauthorized access, mitigating known threats, and filtering traffic before it reaches internal systems. Perimeter firewalls are usually high-performance devices capable of processing large volumes of traffic while applying basic inspection rules.

Beyond the perimeter lies a second layer of firewalls, often referred to as internal or distribution firewalls. These devices are deployed between different internal zones, such as between user networks and data centers, or between development and production environments. Their purpose is to enforce zone-based policies that govern the flow of traffic between different trust levels. For instance, a firewall may permit internal users to access web applications hosted in the DMZ but restrict their access to backend databases. These internal firewalls typically implement more granular policies, including application-layer filtering, user identity awareness, and context-based rules. Because traffic volumes are usually lower than at the perimeter, these firewalls can perform deeper inspection and enforce stricter controls without compromising performance.

A third layer in the hierarchy may include host-based or microsegmentation firewalls, which operate at the level of individual servers, virtual machines, or containers. These firewalls enforce policy at the workload level, controlling not only which services are accessible but also who can access them and under what conditions. Host-based firewalls are particularly useful in environments where lateral movement must be tightly controlled, such as in highly regulated industries or where zero trust principles are applied. In these scenarios, even if an attacker breaches the perimeter or internal firewalls, they are met with additional barriers at the endpoint level, minimizing the risk of data exfiltration or further compromise.

The hierarchical nature of this design enables policies to be enforced progressively as traffic moves deeper into the network. Each layer acts as a checkpoint, applying a specific set of security controls relevant to the context. This approach mirrors the principle of defense in depth, where multiple, redundant layers of security are used to protect critical assets. One key benefit of hierarchical designs is their ability to localize and contain security incidents. If a compromise occurs in one part of the network, internal firewalls can prevent the attacker from accessing other zones. This compartmentalization reduces the potential impact of breaches and supports more efficient incident response.

Hierarchical firewall designs also support scalability by distributing the inspection workload across multiple devices. In traditional single-firewall architectures, all traffic must pass through one device, which can become a bottleneck or single point of failure. In contrast, a hierarchical design spreads the load, allowing each firewall to focus on a specific subset of traffic. This not only improves performance but also enables more precise tuning of policies and inspection engines. Administrators can allocate resources where they are most needed, such as deploying high-throughput devices at the perimeter and more feature-rich appliances in front of critical applications.

Policy management in hierarchical designs requires careful coordination. Each layer must enforce policies that are consistent with overarching security objectives while avoiding redundancy and conflict. Centralized management platforms can assist by providing a unified interface for defining, deploying, and auditing policies across all firewalls in the hierarchy. These platforms allow administrators to apply global rules at the perimeter, zone-specific rules at internal layers, and workload-specific rules at the host level. Such centralized visibility and control are essential for maintaining coherence and ensuring that policies adapt to changes in the environment without creating gaps or overlaps.

Another consideration in hierarchical firewall designs is the integration of logging and monitoring. Because multiple devices are involved in the inspection and enforcement process, it is critical to correlate logs across all layers to gain a complete picture of network activity. Security information and event management systems can aggregate logs from perimeter, internal, and host-level firewalls to detect patterns, track incidents, and identify policy violations. By combining data from different layers, organizations can enhance their ability to detect sophisticated attacks that might evade detection at a single point.

Hierarchical firewall architectures are also well-suited to supporting compliance requirements. Many regulatory frameworks mandate strict segmentation of network resources, detailed logging of access attempts, and layered controls to protect sensitive data. By implementing firewalls at multiple levels, organizations can demonstrate that they have taken comprehensive steps to restrict access and monitor traffic in accordance with regulatory expectations. Furthermore, hierarchical designs facilitate audit readiness by providing clear boundaries and control points that can be independently verified.

The flexibility of hierarchical firewall designs makes them adaptable to a variety of deployment models, including on-premises data centers, hybrid cloud environments, and fully cloud-native architectures. Cloud service providers often offer virtual firewalls and security groups that can be integrated into a hierarchical model, extending policy enforcement into the cloud with the same rigor as in traditional networks. This adaptability ensures that as organizations evolve, their security posture can remain consistent and effective across all platforms and technologies.

In complex and high-risk environments, hierarchical firewall designs provide a structured and scalable way to enforce security policies, control access, and minimize the spread of threats. By placing firewalls at multiple points throughout the network and aligning each with specific zones or functions, organizations gain granular control over how traffic is handled at every stage. This layered approach not only strengthens security but also supports operational efficiency, compliance, and resiliency. As networks continue to expand and threats become more sophisticated, the hierarchical firewall model remains a best practice for designing robust, manageable, and future-ready security architectures.

Multi-Layer Security Implementations

Multi-layer security implementations, often referred to as defense in depth, are a comprehensive approach to network and system protection that relies on deploying multiple, independent layers of security mechanisms throughout an organization's infrastructure. Rather than depending on a single control or security product to prevent breaches, multi-layered security assumes that any single defense can be compromised and therefore supports the idea of redundancy and compartmentalization. By stacking controls across different layers—network, host, application, data, and user—this strategy makes it significantly more difficult for attackers to achieve their objectives, as they must bypass or defeat several layers of defense to reach their target. Each layer provides a unique set of capabilities and is tailored to address specific threats, resulting in a cohesive security posture that is resilient, adaptable, and capable of withstanding diverse attack vectors.

At the outermost layer, network perimeter defenses such as firewalls, intrusion prevention systems, and gateway filters serve as the first line of defense. These systems inspect incoming and outgoing traffic, enforcing policy rules that govern what can enter or leave the network. This layer is essential for blocking known threats, filtering out unwanted traffic, and enforcing access control based on IP addresses, ports, and protocols. However, perimeter defenses alone are insufficient, particularly in modern networks where users and resources are often dispersed across multiple locations, including cloud platforms and remote endpoints. Attackers can bypass the perimeter by compromising internal devices, using stolen credentials, or exploiting misconfigured services, which is why deeper layers of security must be implemented.

The next critical layer lies within internal network segmentation and zone-based control. By breaking up the internal network into discrete zones—such as user, server, management, and DMZ zones—organizations can restrict lateral movement and apply targeted access policies between zones. Firewalls, access control lists, and context-aware security policies govern the traffic that flows between these zones, ensuring that compromised devices cannot freely interact with sensitive systems. This segmentation reduces the attack surface and limits the scope of potential breaches, while also making it easier to monitor and log inter-zone communication for anomaly detection and forensic analysis. Internal segmentation becomes even more powerful when combined with dynamic, context-driven access decisions that incorporate user identity, device status, and location.

Host-based controls form the next layer, focusing on securing individual devices, whether they are servers, desktops, or mobile endpoints. Endpoint protection platforms, host-based firewalls, antivirus software, and device management agents are all part of this layer. These controls enforce local security policies, detect malware, and prevent unauthorized access to system resources. They also support system hardening practices such as patch management, secure configurations, and application whitelisting. Even if an attacker gains network access, host-level controls can prevent privilege escalation or execution of malicious code, serving as a crucial checkpoint that protects critical systems from within. In highly secure environments, these measures may be extended with endpoint detection and response technologies that monitor behavior over time and allow rapid response to threats in real time.

Application security forms another important layer, ensuring that the software and services running on the infrastructure are secure and resilient to exploitation. This includes implementing secure coding practices, performing regular code reviews, and conducting dynamic and static application security testing. Web application firewalls and runtime application self-protection tools can provide real-time enforcement by inspecting application-layer traffic and preventing common attacks such as cross-site scripting, SQL injection, and command injection. Role-based access control within applications ensures that users can only perform actions appropriate to their role, while input validation and session management mechanisms prevent unauthorized manipulation or access. This layer is essential because it directly addresses the services and interfaces that users interact with and that attackers often target.

Data protection is another foundational component of multi-layer security. Encrypting data at rest and in transit ensures that even if it is intercepted or stolen, it cannot be read or modified without proper keys. Data loss prevention systems monitor the movement of sensitive information, ensuring it does not leave the organization inappropriately through email, cloud services, or removable media. Classification systems help organizations understand where sensitive data resides and who has access to it. Backup and recovery solutions further support this layer by providing a mechanism to restore data in the event of ransomware attacks, corruption, or deletion. Strong data security also supports compliance efforts, helping to meet regulatory requirements such as GDPR, HIPAA, or PCI-DSS.

The human element is addressed through the user identity and access management layer. This includes enforcing strong authentication methods, such as multi-factor authentication, to prevent unauthorized access even if credentials are compromised. Centralized identity providers enforce consistent access policies across different systems and environments, while role-based access and the principle of least privilege ensure that users only have access to what they need. Regular review and recertification of user permissions prevent privilege creep and reduce insider threat risks. In addition to technical controls, this layer also encompasses user awareness training, helping employees recognize phishing attempts, social engineering, and unsafe behaviors that could lead to security breaches.

Monitoring and incident response capabilities form a crucial overlay across all security layers. Security information and event management systems collect and correlate data from across the network, detecting patterns that indicate threats and triggering automated responses or alerts. Network and endpoint detection tools complement this effort by analyzing traffic and behavior for signs of compromise. Incident response plans define roles, processes, and escalation paths for handling detected threats, ensuring that responses are coordinated and effective. The ability to quickly detect, contain, and recover from security incidents determines how effectively an organization can withstand a breach and minimize its impact.

In a multi-layer security implementation, integration and coordination between layers is key. Each layer must complement the others, and there must be no blind spots where security is assumed rather than enforced. Communication between tools and the use of centralized policy management systems ensures consistency and visibility. For example, firewall rules should reflect identity-based access policies defined in the IAM system, and endpoint protection alerts should feed into centralized monitoring platforms. When these layers are harmonized, security becomes not just a series of checkpoints, but a cohesive, intelligent framework that adapts to new threats and evolves as the organization changes.

Multi-layer security implementations provide resilience through diversity. Each layer offers a different method of detection or enforcement, targeting specific stages of the attack lifecycle. If one control fails or is bypassed, others are in place to prevent a full compromise. This layered strategy reduces risk, improves visibility, and supports a structured approach to security that aligns with both technical realities and business requirements. In an age where threats are persistent, targeted, and increasingly sophisticated, only a comprehensive, layered security model can offer the depth and adaptability needed to protect the integrity, confidentiality, and availability of critical systems and data.

Scalability and Redundancy in Firewalls

Scalability and redundancy in firewalls are critical principles in the design and maintenance of resilient and high-performance network security infrastructures. As organizations grow and their networks expand to include more users, devices, applications, and services, the firewalls that protect them must be capable of handling increasing traffic volumes and more complex filtering requirements without becoming bottlenecks or points of failure. At the same time, firewalls must be designed with built-in redundancy to ensure that the security perimeter remains intact and functional even in the event of hardware failure, software glitches, or network disruptions. Without scalability, a firewall may not keep up with the demands of a growing business. Without redundancy, a single failure could leave critical assets exposed or disrupt operations entirely. Together, scalability and redundancy form the foundation of a robust firewall deployment that meets the needs of dynamic, mission-critical environments.

Scalability in firewall systems refers to the ability to increase capacity and performance as network demands grow. This can be achieved through vertical or horizontal scaling. Vertical scaling involves upgrading the resources of an existing firewall device, such as adding more processing power, memory, or throughput capacity. While this approach is relatively simple, it has inherent limitations, as there is only so much that a single device can be upgraded before it reaches a ceiling. Horizontal scaling, on the other hand, distributes the traffic load across multiple firewall devices operating in parallel. This method not only provides better scalability but also improves redundancy and fault tolerance. Load balancing technologies are used to distribute incoming and outgoing traffic across a pool of firewalls, ensuring that no single unit becomes a point of congestion or failure.

When scaling firewall deployments, it is essential to consider both control plane and data plane performance. The control plane is responsible for managing connections, enforcing policies, and maintaining session tables, while the data plane handles the actual traffic forwarding and inspection. As traffic increases, both planes must be capable of scaling to prevent delays or dropped connections. Modern firewalls often include hardware acceleration and multi-core processing to improve scalability. These features allow the firewall to inspect more traffic, maintain more concurrent sessions, and enforce more complex rules without degrading performance. Administrators must monitor resource utilization continuously to identify when a firewall is approaching its capacity limits and proactively plan for scaling before issues arise.

Scalability is also a consideration when deploying firewalls in virtualized and cloud environments. Virtual firewalls can be deployed in elastic configurations, automatically spinning up new instances as traffic demands increase and spinning them down when demand falls. This dynamic scalability is especially useful in cloud-native architectures, where traffic patterns can vary dramatically based on time of day, user activity, or workload changes. By integrating firewall scaling with orchestration tools and infrastructure-as-code platforms, organizations can ensure that security enforcement grows in lockstep with their application and service delivery models. These virtualized firewalls must support the same inspection capabilities as their physical counterparts to ensure consistent policy enforcement regardless of the environment.

Redundancy in firewall architecture ensures continuous security enforcement even when individual components fail. High availability configurations are the most common approach to achieving redundancy. In a high availability pair, two firewalls are configured to operate in active-passive or active-active modes. In an active-passive setup, one firewall handles all traffic while the other remains on standby, ready to take over instantly if the active unit fails. In an active-active setup, both firewalls handle traffic simultaneously, providing better resource utilization and load distribution. If one unit fails, the other continues operating without interruption. The choice between active-passive and active-active configurations depends on performance requirements, risk tolerance, and cost considerations.

The effectiveness of a redundant firewall setup depends on the ability of the firewalls to synchronize their state information. For seamless failover, the standby firewall must have up-to-date knowledge of all active sessions, routing tables, and policy rules. Session synchronization is a critical feature that allows ongoing connections to continue without interruption during a failover event. Without it, users may experience dropped sessions, failed transactions, or the need to reconnect. Firewalls that support stateful failover maintain continuous communication between peers, exchanging session data and health checks to ensure readiness and coordination. Administrators must regularly test failover scenarios to validate the effectiveness of redundancy mechanisms and ensure that recovery times meet business continuity requirements.

Redundancy extends beyond the firewall appliances themselves to the surrounding network infrastructure. Multiple network paths, redundant interfaces, and resilient routing protocols contribute to a complete redundant design. Firewalls should be connected to dual upstream routers or switches to avoid single points of failure. In virtualized environments, redundant virtual interfaces and distributed virtual switches help maintain connectivity and failover capabilities. Load balancers can also be part of the redundancy strategy, ensuring that traffic is rerouted to healthy firewall nodes in the event of a failure. Every point of potential failure must be addressed to achieve true redundancy, including power supplies, cabling, and management interfaces.

Scalability and redundancy must also be considered during the policy design phase. As firewall deployments grow and become more distributed, policy management becomes more complex. Centralized policy management platforms help ensure that rules are consistent across multiple firewalls, reducing the risk of configuration drift or conflicting policies. These platforms also simplify the deployment of updates, auditing of rule changes, and enforcement of compliance requirements. Role-based access controls and change control mechanisms add additional layers of governance, helping ensure that scaling and redundancy do not come at the cost of oversight or security discipline.

Monitoring and analytics play a key role in maintaining scalable and redundant firewall environments. Administrators must have real-time visibility into performance metrics, traffic flows, session counts, and failover events. Network telemetry and logging systems provide insights that support capacity planning, fault detection, and incident response. Advanced monitoring tools can detect early warning signs of performance degradation or component failure, allowing preemptive action to avoid service disruption. These tools are also vital for validating that scaling and redundancy mechanisms are working as intended, particularly during high-traffic periods or infrastructure changes.

Designing for scalability and redundancy in firewalls is not simply a matter of adding hardware or duplicating devices. It requires a strategic approach that aligns with the organization's operational needs, growth projections, and risk management goals. Firewalls must be capable of adapting to changing conditions without sacrificing performance or availability. This adaptability involves thoughtful selection of hardware and software, careful planning of network architecture, and disciplined operational practices. The benefits of this approach include uninterrupted security enforcement, better user experiences, improved system resilience, and the ability to support innovation without compromising on protection. In a digital world where uptime and security are equally critical, scalable and redundant firewall designs are no longer optional but essential.

Managing Firewall Policies Over Time

Managing firewall policies over time is a continuous and evolving process that requires strategic oversight, regular reviews, documentation discipline, and the ability to adapt to new business requirements, emerging threats, and evolving network architectures. Firewalls are not static systems; their configurations must evolve alongside changes in organizational structure, application usage, regulatory mandates, and the threat landscape. Without proper policy management, firewalls can become cluttered with outdated rules, misaligned with current operational needs, or weakened by redundant or conflicting entries. This degradation not only affects performance but also introduces significant security risks. Effective firewall policy management ensures that the rules enforced by the firewall remain relevant, optimized, and aligned with the overall security posture of the organization.

The lifecycle of a firewall policy begins with its creation, usually in response to a business requirement or a specific security objective. Policies are developed to define which types of traffic are permitted or denied, under what conditions, and between which sources and destinations. However, the initial deployment of a rule is only the beginning. Over time, applications may be retired, departments may change, and users may relocate or leave the organization. If firewall rules are not reviewed and updated accordingly, they may continue to allow unnecessary or insecure access, or they may block legitimate traffic due to outdated assumptions. Therefore, the management of firewall policies must include a comprehensive change management process that tracks the origin, justification, and approval of each rule, and includes a mechanism for review and retirement.

One of the most persistent challenges in managing firewall policies is rule sprawl. As organizations grow and IT teams respond to ad hoc requests, new rules are often added quickly to meet urgent needs. These additions accumulate over time, often without removing older rules or verifying whether they are still needed. This accumulation leads to long and complex rule sets, which become increasingly difficult to audit, optimize, or troubleshoot. A bloated rule base reduces efficiency because each packet must be evaluated against a larger set of conditions, and it increases the likelihood of overlapping or contradictory rules. Regular policy reviews are necessary to identify rules that are no longer in use, that serve no valid purpose, or that introduce unnecessary risk. Tools that provide visibility into rule usage, hit counts, and redundancy analysis are invaluable for identifying candidates for removal or consolidation.

Documentation is a cornerstone of long-term policy management. Every firewall rule should be associated with metadata that includes a business justification, the name of the requestor, the approval record, and the date of creation. Ideally, this information should also include the expected duration of the rule, especially for temporary access requirements. Without documentation, understanding the intent behind a rule becomes nearly impossible, particularly in environments where staff turnover or organizational restructuring is common. Well-documented policies facilitate audits, support compliance efforts, and streamline the troubleshooting process when access issues or security incidents occur. Centralized policy management systems can help enforce documentation standards and maintain consistency across distributed firewall deployments.

The management process should also incorporate automation where possible. Automated rule analysis tools can identify rules that have not been used in a defined period, rules that conflict with other entries, or rules that are overly permissive. Some tools can simulate traffic against the existing rule set to predict the impact of changes before they are implemented. Automation reduces the risk of human error and accelerates the review process, allowing teams to focus on high-priority issues rather than manually inspecting every rule. However, automation should not replace human oversight entirely. Each proposed change should still be reviewed by knowledgeable security professionals to ensure it aligns with broader organizational policies and does not introduce unintended vulnerabilities.

Another vital aspect of managing firewall policies is aligning them with organizational changes. As departments merge, new business units are created, or cloud services are adopted, firewall policies must be updated to reflect new traffic flows and access requirements. Policies that once applied to on-premises servers may need to be replicated in cloud environments or integrated with virtual firewalls. As organizations embrace hybrid or multi-cloud architectures, the consistency of firewall policies across platforms becomes a concern. Policy management must account for differences in technology, capabilities, and administrative models between on-premises and cloud-based firewalls. Adopting a policy-as-code approach can help bridge these gaps, allowing policies to be defined in a platform-neutral format and deployed consistently through automation pipelines.

Security audits and regulatory compliance play a strong role in shaping long-term policy management. Many regulations require evidence of access controls, regular reviews of security policies, and documentation of changes. Managing firewall policies in this context involves generating reports that demonstrate compliance, retaining logs of changes and justifications, and proving that access rules are reviewed on a scheduled basis. These activities should not be treated as one-time efforts but as part of a continuous improvement cycle that reinforces the relevance and accuracy of firewall configurations. Audit readiness should be a natural outcome of well-managed policies, not a burdensome last-minute scramble.

Testing and validation are also critical. Every time a firewall policy is added, removed, or modified, it must be validated to ensure it behaves as intended. This includes confirming that permitted traffic flows correctly, that blocked traffic is indeed denied, and that no other rules are inadvertently affected. In complex environments, test environments or rule simulation tools can be used to evaluate the effects of a change before it is pushed to production. Change windows and rollback procedures must also be in place to minimize disruption in the event of unexpected behavior.

Training and coordination across teams play a major role in sustaining long-term policy management. Network engineers, security analysts, and application owners must communicate effectively to ensure that firewall policies reflect both security requirements and operational needs. Firewalls should not be viewed as isolated technical components but as active participants in the organization's security framework. Security teams must foster a culture in which access requests are scrutinized, temporary permissions are tracked and removed, and policy ownership is clearly defined.

Managing firewall policies over time is an evolving responsibility that requires strategic planning, disciplined execution, and continuous improvement. It is not simply about writing and enforcing rules but about aligning those rules with real-world needs, adapting them to changing environments, and ensuring that they remain effective, efficient, and compliant. A well-managed firewall is not just a static gatekeeper but a dynamic instrument of security governance that reflects the organization's values, priorities, and risk tolerance. As threats grow more sophisticated and infrastructures more complex, the ability to manage firewall policies proactively and effectively becomes a defining factor in the resilience and reliability of any enterprise network.

Dynamic Security Policies and Automation

Dynamic security policies and automation have become essential in modern network environments that demand speed, flexibility, and resilience. Traditional static security models, which rely on fixed rules and manual configurations, are increasingly insufficient to keep pace with the rapid evolution of applications, users, devices, and threats. In contrast, dynamic security policies respond to changes in the environment automatically, adjusting access controls, inspection rules, and enforcement mechanisms based on real-time data and contextual information. Automation amplifies this capability by enabling security tools and systems to make decisions, apply configurations, and coordinate responses without direct human intervention. Together, dynamic policies and automation create a living security architecture that is adaptive, responsive, and capable of protecting complex and fluid infrastructures.

A dynamic security policy is one that adapts based on conditions such as user identity, device posture, location, time of day, behavioral patterns, or threat intelligence feeds. Rather than applying the same rules to all users and systems at all times, dynamic policies tailor enforcement to the specific context of a request or activity. For example, a user accessing a sensitive application from a corporate laptop on the internal network during business hours might be granted full access, while the same user connecting from an unknown device or external location at night might receive restricted access or be denied entirely. This flexibility allows organizations to implement more nuanced and risk-aware controls, reducing unnecessary friction for legitimate users while strengthening defenses against suspicious or unauthorized behavior.

Dynamic policies are often built on top of identity and access management frameworks that provide centralized control over user credentials, roles, and attributes. These attributes, including group membership, job function, department, and security clearance, can be used as criteria for security decisions. Integration with directory services, authentication platforms, and single sign-on solutions allows security systems to dynamically evaluate access requests against policy conditions. When combined with endpoint detection tools that assess device health and compliance, such as the presence of antivirus software or recent security patches, dynamic policies can enforce conditional access based on a comprehensive understanding of risk.

Automation plays a key role in enabling and enforcing dynamic security policies. Manual configuration of firewall rules, access control lists, or application permissions for every change in user behavior or network condition would be impractical and error-prone. Automation eliminates this burden by translating policy logic into executable workflows that respond instantly to events. For instance, when a user is added to a sensitive project team in a human resources application, automation can update firewall rules, assign appropriate network segmentation, and provision application access based on predefined templates. Similarly, if an endpoint is detected as compromised, automation can isolate it from the network, revoke credentials, and trigger alerts without waiting for manual intervention.

Orchestration platforms are central to implementing automated security policies. These platforms coordinate actions across multiple systems, including firewalls, intrusion detection systems, access gateways, cloud security groups, and endpoint agents. They provide a single source of truth for policy definitions and use APIs to push configurations to all relevant devices and services. This coordination ensures consistency and reduces the likelihood of configuration drift or conflicting rules across environments. It also allows for complex policy logic that spans multiple domains, such as blocking traffic to certain IP addresses only if it originates from a particular user group and is detected during a predefined risk period.

One of the most transformative aspects of dynamic policy automation is its ability to incorporate real-time threat intelligence. Security systems can subscribe to feeds that provide updated lists of malicious IPs, domains, file hashes, or attack indicators. As new threats are discovered, these indicators can be automatically incorporated into policies that block traffic, quarantine affected assets, or trigger additional inspections. This responsiveness drastically reduces the window of exposure to new and evolving threats, making it more difficult for attackers to exploit vulnerabilities before defenses are updated. Threat intelligence integration also enables predictive defenses that identify emerging attack patterns and apply preemptive countermeasures.

In cloud environments, dynamic security policies are especially critical. Cloud workloads are highly dynamic by nature, with instances spinning up and down, services moving between availability zones, and users accessing resources from various locations. Security groups and access rules must adjust automatically to accommodate this fluidity without compromising control. Infrastructure as code plays a key role in this context, allowing security policies to be defined as code alongside network and compute configurations. These policies can be versioned, tested, and deployed through automated pipelines, ensuring that security enforcement keeps pace with infrastructure changes. When an application is deployed, the appropriate security rules are deployed with it, reducing reliance on manual rule creation and minimizing the risk of oversights.

Machine learning and behavioral analytics further enhance the power of dynamic and automated security. By analyzing normal activity patterns over time, these systems can identify deviations that suggest compromise, misuse, or insider threats. When such anomalies are detected, automated workflows can apply dynamic policies that restrict access, increase monitoring, or escalate incidents for human review. For example, if a user who typically accesses files from a single department suddenly attempts to download large datasets from multiple departments, an automated policy could block the activity and notify the security team. These intelligent responses are essential in detecting sophisticated threats that evade signature-based detection or occur slowly over time.

While the benefits of dynamic policies and automation are substantial, their implementation must be approached with care. Policies must be thoroughly defined, tested, and monitored to ensure they behave as intended. Misconfigured automation can result in unintended access, service disruptions, or even lockout scenarios that affect critical operations. Security teams must maintain visibility into automated actions, with logging, alerting, and rollback mechanisms in place to support auditing and recovery. Governance structures must be established to oversee policy changes, validate policy effectiveness, and manage exceptions in a controlled manner. Training and awareness are also important, as security staff must shift from a reactive mindset to a proactive and automation-driven approach.

Dynamic security policies and automation are not just enhancements to traditional security models but represent a fundamental shift in how security is enforced in modern environments. They enable organizations to respond to threats faster, enforce policies with greater precision, and scale protections across complex and distributed infrastructures. By leveraging contextual awareness, orchestration, and intelligence-driven decisions, dynamic security policies transform static, brittle defenses into adaptive and resilient systems. As the digital landscape continues to expand and threats grow more complex, the ability to automatically adjust defenses in real time will be a defining characteristic of effective cybersecurity programs. Embracing automation and dynamic policies is not merely a technological upgrade—it is a strategic imperative for maintaining security, agility, and competitiveness in the face of constant change.

Access Control in Virtualized Environments

Access control in virtualized environments introduces a new dimension of complexity and flexibility in network and system security. As organizations increasingly shift to virtualized infrastructure to support scalability, agility, and cost efficiency, the traditional models of access control that relied on physical network perimeters and static configurations must evolve. Virtualization abstracts the underlying hardware and allows workloads, applications, and storage to be dynamically provisioned, moved, or decommissioned. In such a fluid environment, maintaining effective access control becomes a dynamic challenge. Security policies must not only protect virtual machines and containers but also extend to virtual switches, hypervisors, management consoles, and orchestration tools. Ensuring that only authorized entities can interact with these components requires a rethinking of conventional access control strategies and the adoption of virtualization-aware security controls.

In a virtualized data center, the concept of perimeter is significantly blurred. Multiple virtual machines may reside on the same physical host, each with its own operating system, applications, and network interfaces. These VMs may belong to different departments, serve distinct purposes, or operate under varying compliance requirements. Without proper access control, one compromised VM could potentially be used as a pivot point to access others on the same host. Traditional firewalls that operate at the physical network layer are not equipped to distinguish between inter-VM traffic on the same host. To address this limitation, access control must be enforced at the hypervisor level or through virtualized network components such as distributed virtual switches and software-defined firewalls.

Hypervisor-based access control plays a central role in securing virtual environments. The hypervisor is the underlying software layer that allows multiple virtual machines to run on a single physical server. Because it controls the allocation of hardware resources and mediates communication between VMs and the network, the hypervisor must enforce strict isolation between tenants and workloads. Administrators must implement role-based access controls for the hypervisor management interface, ensuring that only authorized personnel can perform operations such as creating, deleting, or modifying virtual machines. Access to the management API, which is often used by orchestration tools, must be secured using strong authentication mechanisms and encrypted communication channels to prevent unauthorized manipulation of the virtual infrastructure.

Virtualized network access control requires visibility into east-west traffic, which refers to communication between virtual machines within the same data center or host. This traffic is often not visible to traditional perimeter defenses, making it a potential blind spot for attackers. To mitigate this risk, organizations deploy microsegmentation, a technique that applies fine-grained access control policies to individual workloads or logical groupings of workloads. Microsegmentation allows administrators to define who can talk to whom within the virtual environment, based on factors such as application role, security zone, or compliance domain. These policies are enforced by virtual firewalls or security groups that are integrated with the virtualization platform. Because policies are abstracted from physical infrastructure, they can move with the workload, maintaining consistent enforcement even when VMs are migrated between hosts.

Access control in virtualized environments must also account for orchestration and automation tools, which play a significant role in provisioning and managing infrastructure. Platforms such as VMware vSphere, Microsoft Hyper-V, and cloud-native orchestrators like Kubernetes and OpenStack provide APIs and dashboards that allow administrators to control the lifecycle of virtual machines and containers. These tools must be secured with access controls that follow the principle of least privilege, granting users and service accounts only the permissions necessary to perform their functions. Multi-factor authentication and detailed audit logging should be implemented to monitor administrative actions and detect potential misuse. Orchestration platforms must also enforce access boundaries between tenants or projects, preventing accidental or malicious cross-tenant access.

Containerized environments introduce further challenges and opportunities for access control. Containers share the same operating system kernel and often run in high-density configurations, which can lead to increased attack surfaces if not properly isolated. Access control in containerized environments must extend to the runtime engine, image repositories, and orchestrators such as Kubernetes. Policies should govern who can deploy or modify containers, which images are permitted, and what network or storage resources containers can access. Kubernetes, for example, supports role-based access control, network policies, and admission controllers to enforce granular access rules. These controls must be continuously monitored and updated as workloads change and new components are added to the environment.

Storage access control is another critical aspect of virtualized security. Virtual machines rely on shared storage systems for their disk images, snapshots, and backups. Unauthorized access to these storage systems can result in data theft, loss, or corruption. Access controls should be applied at the storage controller and hypervisor level to ensure that only designated virtual machines or management systems can access specific volumes. Encryption at rest and in transit, combined with access auditing, provides additional layers of protection. In multi-tenant environments, logical isolation of storage is necessary to prevent leakage between customers or departments.

A successful access control strategy in virtualized environments must be integrated with centralized identity and policy management systems. This integration allows for consistent policy enforcement across physical and virtual resources and enables the use of dynamic access policies based on user roles, device attributes, or security posture. Identity federation and single sign-on mechanisms help unify access control across hybrid environments, allowing administrators to apply consistent policies whether a workload resides in a private data center or a public cloud. These capabilities support the implementation of zero trust architectures, where every request is authenticated, authorized, and inspected regardless of origin.

Monitoring and auditing are indispensable components of access control in virtualized infrastructures. Because changes can occur rapidly and dynamically, organizations must maintain visibility into who is accessing what, when, and how. Security information and event management systems can collect logs from hypervisors, virtual switches, orchestration platforms, and firewalls to provide a holistic view of access activity. These logs should be analyzed in real time to detect anomalies, such as unusual login attempts, privilege escalations, or unexpected network flows between workloads. Automated responses, such as revoking credentials or isolating suspicious VMs, enhance the responsiveness of the access control framework.

Access control in virtualized environments requires a multilayered approach that encompasses users, systems, networks, and workloads. It must be dynamic, context-aware, and capable of adapting to the ever-changing nature of virtual infrastructure. By leveraging native virtualization security features, integrating with centralized identity systems, enforcing microsegmentation, and continuously monitoring access events, organizations can build a resilient access control model that supports operational agility without compromising security. As virtualization technologies continue to evolve and form the foundation of modern IT architectures, access control strategies must evolve with them to remain effective and aligned with the broader goals of confidentiality, integrity, and availability.

Traffic Control in Cloud Infrastructure

Traffic control in cloud infrastructure has become a fundamental component of modern network security and operational efficiency. As enterprises increasingly migrate workloads to public, private, or hybrid clouds, they encounter a fundamentally different environment than traditional on-premises networks. In the cloud, infrastructure is abstracted, dynamic, and highly automated, which requires a reimagining of how traffic is monitored, filtered, segmented, and prioritized. Unlike static physical networks where administrators have granular control over every device and connection, cloud environments rely on virtual networking components such as security groups, network access control lists, virtual private clouds, and software-defined networking. These constructs must be meticulously configured and continuously managed to enforce traffic control policies effectively. The challenge lies in balancing accessibility and performance with security, visibility, and compliance in an environment where changes can occur rapidly and at scale.

One of the foundational elements of traffic control in the cloud is the concept of virtual network segmentation. Cloud service providers offer virtual networks that can be divided into subnets, each with its own route tables, access controls, and gateways. Administrators use these segments to isolate workloads based on function, sensitivity, or exposure to the internet. For example, a public-facing web server might reside in a subnet with inbound access from the internet, while backend databases are placed in private subnets with no direct external connectivity. Traffic between these subnets is controlled using cloud-native mechanisms such as security groups and network ACLs. Security groups act as virtual firewalls attached to individual instances, defining which types of traffic are allowed in or out based on IP address, protocol, and port. These controls are stateful, meaning return traffic is automatically permitted. Network ACLs, on the other hand, operate at the subnet level and are stateless, requiring explicit rules for both inbound and outbound traffic.

Beyond basic segmentation, advanced traffic control in cloud environments involves microsegmentation. This approach applies fine-grained policies to control traffic between workloads even within the same subnet or security zone. Microsegmentation is essential in enforcing least-privilege access models and preventing lateral movement by attackers who may compromise a single workload. In cloud environments, microsegmentation can be implemented using host-based firewalls, service mesh architectures, or third-party security appliances integrated into the virtual network. These solutions monitor and enforce traffic flows at the application level, enabling policy enforcement based on attributes such as workload identity, application type, or user context. This depth of control helps enforce compliance standards and supports zero trust architectures, where no implicit trust is given based on network location alone.

Traffic control also encompasses ingress and egress filtering. Ingress filtering involves managing and inspecting traffic entering the cloud environment, typically through internet gateways, load balancers, or VPN endpoints. Policies at this level determine which sources can initiate connections and under what conditions. Egress filtering controls traffic leaving the cloud environment, preventing unauthorized data exfiltration, enforcing acceptable use policies, and restricting communication with known malicious destinations. Egress controls are particularly important for cloud workloads that access external APIs, cloud services, or third-party platforms. Misconfigured egress rules can result in significant data leakage or compliance violations. Effective traffic control strategies employ both ingress and egress rules in a layered manner, ensuring that traffic is verified and filtered at every stage of its journey.

Traffic control must also account for multi-region and multi-cloud architectures. Organizations often deploy workloads across multiple geographic regions to improve availability, reduce latency, or meet data sovereignty requirements. In such configurations, traffic control policies must be synchronized across regions and enforced consistently to prevent configuration drift. Cloud-native solutions like transit gateways, inter-region peering, and centralized routing policies help facilitate secure and efficient traffic flow between regions. In multi-cloud environments, where different providers may use different constructs and terminology, centralized policy management and automation tools are necessary to maintain consistency. These tools abstract the differences between cloud providers and allow administrators to define traffic control policies in a unified language that is deployed across all platforms.

Visibility is another critical component of effective traffic control in cloud infrastructure. Unlike traditional networks where administrators can tap into physical links and mirror traffic, cloud environments require reliance on logs, flow data, and monitoring services provided by the cloud vendor. For example, services like AWS VPC Flow Logs, Azure NSG Flow Logs, or Google Cloud VPC Flow Logs provide records of allowed and denied traffic at the interface level. These logs must be collected, analyzed, and correlated with other telemetry data to identify anomalies, troubleshoot connectivity issues, and validate policy effectiveness. Network monitoring tools designed for the cloud can provide real-time dashboards, alerting, and traffic analytics that support incident response and performance optimization.

Another aspect of traffic control is quality of service and bandwidth management. Although most public cloud providers do not expose traditional QoS configuration to customers in the same way as enterprise routers or switches, some level of traffic prioritization is still possible through architectural decisions. For example, separating latency-sensitive workloads into dedicated subnets, using high-throughput instance types, or leveraging load balancers with intelligent routing algorithms can help manage performance. Cloud providers also offer traffic shaping and rate limiting features at the application layer or through APIs to control the volume of requests and prevent abuse. These controls are especially important in multi-tenant environments or applications that serve public users at scale.

Automation is essential to managing traffic control policies in dynamic cloud environments. Infrastructure as code allows organizations to define and version their network policies alongside application code, enabling consistent deployment and easier rollback. Changes to traffic control settings can be integrated into CI/CD pipelines, automatically applied during environment provisioning, or validated during testing phases. Policy-as-code frameworks extend this concept by enabling the definition of security and traffic policies in declarative syntax, which can be audited, enforced, and automatically remediated when drift is detected. Automation reduces the chance of human error and accelerates response times to new business or security requirements.

In a cloud-native world, traffic control is not a one-time configuration but an ongoing process that must adapt to changes in workload placement, user behavior, threat landscape, and regulatory obligations. Security teams must continuously evaluate and refine traffic control policies to ensure they remain effective and aligned with business goals. This includes regular reviews of rules, removal of obsolete entries, validation of least-privilege models, and incorporation of threat intelligence to dynamically adjust access policies. Collaboration between networking, security, and development teams is also essential to ensure that traffic control policies support, rather than hinder, innovation and service delivery.

Traffic control in cloud infrastructure requires a shift in mindset, moving away from rigid perimeter defenses and toward flexible, context-aware policies that are embedded throughout the network fabric. It involves a combination of segmentation, microsegmentation, ingress and egress filtering, visibility, and automation, all operating in concert to protect assets and ensure efficient, secure communications. As organizations continue to adopt cloud at scale, the ability to implement, manage, and evolve traffic control mechanisms will become a defining capability of secure and resilient cloud operations. The complexity of cloud environments demands that traffic control not only be technically sound but also intelligently designed to align with modern architectures and security strategies.

Integrating Firewalls with SDN

Integrating firewalls with software-defined networking represents a critical advancement in the evolution of network security and control. Software-defined networking, or SDN, introduces a paradigm shift in how networks are managed, replacing traditional hardware-centric models with programmable, centralized control. In an SDN architecture, the control plane is decoupled from the data plane, allowing network behavior to be dynamically adjusted through software. This centralization enables administrators to manage large, distributed environments from a single point of control. However, while SDN brings agility, scalability, and automation, it also introduces new challenges in enforcing consistent security policies across highly dynamic and abstracted network environments. Firewalls, traditionally deployed at fixed points in the network, must be reengineered to align with the flexibility and programmability of SDN. The integration of firewalls into SDN must therefore be seamless, policy-driven, and capable of real-time response to network changes.

In a conventional network, firewalls are positioned at the perimeter or between major network segments, where they inspect traffic and enforce security rules based on static configurations. These rules are typically based on IP addresses, port numbers, and protocol types. In an SDN environment, where endpoints and services are frequently provisioned, moved, or terminated, static firewall rules quickly become obsolete or misaligned with actual network behavior. The dynamic nature of SDN demands that firewalls become equally dynamic, capable of adjusting their enforcement logic based on real-time changes in the network topology, flow behavior, and policy context. This requires deep integration between the SDN controller and the firewall system, allowing the controller to orchestrate not only forwarding behavior but also security enforcement.

One of the primary benefits of integrating firewalls with SDN is the ability to implement intent-based security policies. Rather than configuring firewalls individually with detailed rule sets, administrators can define high-level security intents, such as allowing specific types of communication between application tiers or restricting access to sensitive resources. These intents are interpreted by the SDN controller, which then programs the underlying infrastructure—including firewalls—with the necessary configurations to enforce the desired behavior. This abstraction significantly reduces complexity and ensures that security policies are consistently applied across the network, regardless of how workloads are deployed or moved. Firewalls become part of an automated enforcement fabric, capable of adapting to changes without manual intervention.

SDN-integrated firewalls also enable more granular and context-aware security. In traditional models, firewall rules are based on relatively static attributes like IP addresses or subnets. In SDN, security policies can leverage dynamic context such as user identity, application type, device status, or even behavioral analytics. For example, a policy might permit access to a database only if the request originates from a known application server running on a compliant host and associated with an authenticated user. This level of granularity is possible because the

SDN controller maintains a global view of the network and can correlate information from multiple sources, including identity systems, endpoint protection platforms, and threat intelligence feeds. Firewalls, when integrated into this framework, enforce policies that reflect not just where traffic is coming from, but also who is sending it and under what conditions.

Another key aspect of integration is the ability to dynamically insert firewall functions into traffic flows as needed. In traditional networks, firewalls are statically placed and all traffic must be routed through them, which can lead to bottlenecks and inefficient routing. In an SDN environment, service chaining allows specific security services to be dynamically applied to traffic based on policy. For instance, a web request from an untrusted network might be directed through a chain that includes a firewall, a web application firewall, and an intrusion prevention system. If the traffic is from a trusted source and targeting a non-sensitive application, it might bypass certain inspection stages. This flexibility optimizes performance while ensuring that security is applied where it is most needed. The SDN controller orchestrates these flows in real time, directing packets through the appropriate service paths based on policy and context.

To achieve seamless integration, firewalls must support APIs and protocols that allow interaction with SDN controllers. OpenFlow, RESTful APIs, and vendor-specific extensions are commonly used to facilitate communication between the control plane and the firewall services. Firewalls that expose programmable interfaces can be dynamically configured by the controller, enabling real-time updates to rules, inspection profiles, and logging behavior. This programmability also supports automation workflows, where security responses to detected threats—such as quarantining a compromised host or blocking a suspicious domain—can be implemented instantly without manual intervention. Firewalls become responsive elements in an adaptive security architecture, capable of taking immediate action based on events and conditions observed elsewhere in the network.

Monitoring and visibility are enhanced when firewalls are integrated into the SDN framework. The centralized nature of SDN allows administrators to view and analyze network traffic from a global perspective, including the enforcement points within the firewall infrastructure. Logs, alerts, and telemetry from firewalls can be correlated with data from the SDN controller, enabling faster incident detection and more accurate root cause analysis. When a security incident occurs, administrators can trace the path of the affected flows, identify which policies were applied, and determine what actions were taken by the firewall. This level of insight is crucial for compliance, audit readiness, and proactive threat hunting.

However, integrating firewalls with SDN also introduces new challenges. The centralization of control increases the potential impact of misconfigurations or compromises. If the SDN controller is breached or malfunctioning, it could misconfigure firewalls across the entire network, potentially exposing sensitive data or allowing malicious traffic. Therefore, securing the SDN control plane is of paramount importance. Strong authentication, role-based access control, encryption of controller communications, and rigorous change management procedures must be in place to protect the integrity of the system. Additionally, firewall policies must be carefully validated and tested, as the automation and dynamic nature of SDN can rapidly propagate errors if not properly constrained.

As organizations adopt more sophisticated network architectures, including hybrid cloud, edge computing, and multi-tenant environments, the integration of firewalls with SDN becomes not just beneficial but necessary. It allows for scalable, adaptable, and efficient security enforcement that keeps pace with the speed of business and technology change. By combining the centralized intelligence of SDN with the inspection and enforcement capabilities of modern firewalls, organizations can achieve a level of security control that is both comprehensive and responsive. The result is a network that not only moves faster but also defends itself more effectively, adapting in real time to new users, applications, and threats. In a world where agility and security must go hand in hand, the integration of firewalls with software-defined networking is a cornerstone of the future of secure networking.

Threat Detection and Prevention via Filtering

Threat detection and prevention via filtering is one of the most foundational yet constantly evolving pillars of network security. Filtering mechanisms are deployed throughout an organization's infrastructure to monitor, evaluate, and control the flow of data, making real-time decisions about whether to allow or block traffic based on defined security policies and observed behavior. Filtering is not just about rejecting malicious packets; it plays a crucial role in identifying suspicious activity, enforcing compliance, and preventing lateral movement within networks. As cyber threats become more sophisticated and stealthy, the effectiveness of filtering technologies in detecting and mitigating these threats has become critical to maintaining the integrity and availability of information systems.

At its core, filtering is about scrutinizing network traffic against a set of rules or behavioral models. These rules can be simple, such as blocking known malicious IP addresses or denying traffic on certain ports, or they can be complex, involving deep packet inspection, content analysis, and anomaly detection. Traditional packet filtering operates at the network and transport layers, evaluating headers for source and destination addresses, port numbers, and protocol types. While this type of filtering is still useful for enforcing basic access control, it is insufficient against modern threats that operate at the application layer or leverage encrypted traffic to conceal malicious payloads. Therefore, filtering technologies must evolve to include more context-aware and content-sensitive methods of inspection.

Stateful inspection represents a significant advancement over stateless packet filtering. By keeping track of the state of active connections, stateful firewalls can determine whether a packet is part of an established session or a suspicious unsolicited attempt to initiate communication. This capability is essential for distinguishing legitimate traffic from scanning activity or connection hijacking. Furthermore, stateful filtering supports dynamic policy enforcement, allowing temporary rules to be created in response to approved connection requests and automatically removed when the session ends. This approach minimizes the attack surface and reduces the risk of misconfiguration that could result in persistent access paths for attackers.

Another powerful layer of threat detection via filtering is deep packet inspection. DPI goes beyond header information and examines the payload of packets, enabling the detection of threats that are embedded within otherwise benign traffic. For example, DPI can identify malware hidden in file transfers, detect command-and-control messages within HTTP requests, or recognize data exfiltration attempts disguised as DNS queries. By analyzing content in real time, DPI allows for immediate prevention actions such as dropping the packet, resetting the session, or alerting security teams. DPI is especially valuable in environments where encrypted traffic is terminated and inspected by next-generation firewalls or intrusion prevention systems, revealing threats that would otherwise be invisible to traditional filters.

Behavioral filtering adds another dimension to threat detection by establishing a baseline of normal network activity and identifying deviations that may indicate compromise. Instead of relying solely on signature-based detection, behavioral filters use algorithms and machine learning models to recognize patterns that deviate from historical norms. This includes unusual login attempts, sudden spikes in data transfer, access to previously unused services, or communication with unfamiliar hosts. These indicators of compromise often precede a full-scale attack or data breach and can provide early warning that enables containment before damage occurs. Behavioral filtering is particularly effective in detecting zero-day attacks and advanced persistent threats that are designed to bypass known defenses.

Application-aware filtering further refines threat detection capabilities by understanding the context and structure of specific applications. Modern firewalls can identify traffic not only by port and protocol but also by application type, user identity, and usage behavior. This allows administrators to create policies that permit specific actions within applications while blocking others. For example, it may be acceptable for users to access a cloud storage service but not to upload files to it. Application-aware filters can enforce such granular controls, reducing the risk of data loss and preventing misuse of legitimate services as vectors for attack. Additionally, by integrating with directory services, application-aware filters can enforce role-based policies, allowing different levels of access based on user roles or departments.

Threat intelligence feeds play a crucial role in enhancing filtering capabilities by providing real-time data about emerging threats. These feeds supply continuously updated lists of known malicious IP addresses, domain names, URLs, and file hashes that filters can use to block traffic associated with threat actors. Integration with threat intelligence platforms allows filters to respond dynamically to the global threat landscape, preventing access to command-and-control servers, phishing websites, or malware distribution points before they can impact the organization. Some advanced filtering systems can even share local threat intelligence findings with global networks, contributing to collective defense efforts across multiple organizations and industries.

Filtering technologies are also central to preventing insider threats and enforcing data loss prevention policies. By monitoring outbound traffic, filters can detect attempts to transfer sensitive information outside the organization, whether through email, cloud storage, or web uploads. Content filtering engines inspect data for patterns such as credit card numbers, personal identification, or confidential documents and can block, quarantine, or log these activities. In regulated industries, this capability supports compliance with standards such as GDPR, HIPAA, or PCI-DSS. It also helps ensure that employees, whether negligent or malicious, cannot compromise the confidentiality of critical data assets.

In cloud and hybrid environments, filtering must extend beyond traditional perimeters to cover traffic between cloud workloads, between on-premises and cloud systems, and across distributed architectures. Virtual firewalls, cloud-native security groups, and workload-level inspection agents provide filtering capabilities that follow workloads wherever they are deployed. These filters must be centrally managed and policy-driven to ensure consistency across environments. They must also be able to inspect encrypted traffic, apply context-aware rules, and scale automatically in response to dynamic changes in cloud workloads. The integration of filtering with orchestration platforms and infrastructure-as-code tools further enables the rapid deployment of security controls that are aligned with DevOps practices.

While filtering provides robust mechanisms for detecting and blocking threats, it must also be continuously monitored and refined. Threat actors are constantly developing evasion techniques to bypass filtering mechanisms, such as using encryption, polymorphism, or protocol tunneling. Security teams must regularly review filter configurations, update signatures and models, and validate the effectiveness of rules through testing and simulation. Logging and alerting from filters must be integrated with security information and event management systems to provide holistic visibility and support rapid response. Metrics such as rule hit counts, blocked session statistics, and false positive rates are essential for tuning filters to balance security and usability.

Threat detection and prevention through filtering is an indispensable component of modern cybersecurity architectures. It provides a real-time shield against a wide range of attack vectors and enables organizations to enforce security policies with precision and confidence. By combining stateful inspection, deep packet analysis, behavioral analytics, application awareness, and threat intelligence, filtering technologies offer comprehensive protection against both known and unknown threats. Their adaptability, scalability, and integration with broader security ecosystems ensure that they remain relevant and effective in an ever-changing digital landscape. As attackers become more innovative, the filtering strategies used to detect and prevent threats must become equally intelligent, proactive, and deeply embedded in the fabric of network and information security.

Compliance Considerations in Access Control

Compliance considerations in access control have become a defining concern for organizations operating in a landscape increasingly shaped by regulatory scrutiny, data protection obligations, and industry-specific standards. Access control is not only a security function but also a legal and operational necessity that directly affects how organizations manage their sensitive information, ensure the privacy of users and customers, and demonstrate accountability to regulators. Regulatory frameworks around the world mandate that organizations implement effective access controls to protect data confidentiality, integrity, and availability. These controls must be well-documented, regularly reviewed, and auditable. Failure to comply can result in significant fines, reputational damage, and loss of customer trust. Therefore, aligning access control practices with compliance requirements is a strategic imperative that demands attention to technical, procedural, and organizational factors.

Access control mechanisms must first address the fundamental principle of least privilege. This principle dictates that users, systems, and processes should have only the minimum access necessary to perform their roles or functions. Regulatory frameworks such as the General Data Protection Regulation, the Health Insurance Portability and Accountability Act, and the Payment Card Industry Data Security Standard explicitly require the enforcement of least privilege as a core component of data protection. Implementing this principle involves role-based access control models, where permissions are assigned based on the responsibilities associated with specific job functions. It also requires strong identity and access management systems that can authenticate users, assign appropriate roles, and enforce these roles across multiple applications and systems. Compliance is not just about the technical implementation of controls but also about demonstrating that access decisions are justified, documented, and periodically revalidated.

Segregation of duties is another critical compliance consideration. It is designed to prevent conflicts of interest and reduce the risk of fraud or abuse by ensuring that no single individual has control over all aspects of a sensitive process. For example, a user who can both initiate and approve financial transactions poses a compliance risk. Access control systems must support the enforcement of segregation policies by defining access rules that prevent such combinations of permissions. This often requires collaboration between IT, HR, and compliance departments to map business processes, identify critical control points, and assign access accordingly. Auditors often focus on segregation of duties as part of their review, and organizations must be able to produce evidence that these policies are enforced and monitored.

Auditability and traceability are essential for proving compliance. Regulators require organizations to maintain records of who accessed what data, when, and for what purpose. Access control systems must generate logs that capture authentication events, access attempts, privilege escalations, and configuration changes. These logs must be protected from tampering, retained for a prescribed period, and made available for review upon request. Compliance frameworks often specify log retention requirements and define what information must be included in audit trails. For example, under Sarbanes-Oxley regulations, public companies must maintain detailed access logs related to financial systems to ensure that financial reporting is accurate and protected from manipulation. Automated logging tools integrated with centralized security information and event management platforms help organizations meet these requirements while providing real-time visibility into potential compliance violations.

Access reviews and recertifications are recurring obligations in many compliance regimes. These processes involve regularly reviewing user accounts and their assigned permissions to ensure that they are still appropriate. Changes in job roles, project assignments, or employment status can render previous access assignments obsolete or excessive. Without regular reviews, organizations run the risk of privilege creep, where users accumulate access rights over time beyond what is necessary for their current role. Regulations such as ISO/IEC 27001 and NIST 800-53 emphasize the importance of periodic access reviews to maintain a secure and compliant environment. These reviews must be documented and often require managerial approval, forming part of the overall governance of access control. Automation tools can assist in scheduling and executing reviews, generating reports, and tracking follow-up actions for non-compliant accounts.

Data classification also influences compliance in access control. Not all data is subject to the same level of regulatory protection, so access control policies must reflect the sensitivity of the information being protected. For example, personally identifiable information, payment card data, and protected health information are subject to specific compliance requirements that may not apply to general business documents. By classifying data according to its regulatory significance, organizations can apply more stringent access controls to sensitive information while maintaining usability and efficiency for less critical data. Data classification schemes must be consistently applied and supported by labeling tools, user training, and technical enforcement mechanisms that restrict access based on classification labels.

Cross-border data access presents additional compliance challenges. Many regulations place restrictions on where data can be stored or accessed, particularly when it comes to transferring personal data across international boundaries. For example, the GDPR imposes strict rules on the transfer of data from the European Economic Area to countries without adequate data protection laws. Access control systems must be capable of enforcing geographic restrictions, preventing users in unauthorized jurisdictions from accessing certain types of data. This may involve geo-fencing, IP filtering, or location-aware access policies that dynamically evaluate the origin of an access request before granting permission. Organizations must also track and report on cross-border access as part of their compliance obligations.

Vendor and third-party access is another critical area requiring compliance-focused controls. Many organizations rely on external partners, contractors, and service providers who need access to internal systems and data. Compliance frameworks mandate that such access be carefully controlled, monitored, and limited in scope and duration. Contracts must include data protection clauses, and technical controls must enforce the principle of least privilege for external users. Temporary access should be automatically revoked after predefined periods, and all third-party activity should be logged and subject to audit. Failure to properly manage third-party access has been the root cause of several high-profile data breaches, making it a focal point for compliance audits and risk assessments.

Access control policies must be documented, communicated, and enforced as part of a broader compliance strategy. Policies should define who is responsible for managing access, how access is granted and revoked, what constitutes acceptable use, and how violations are handled. These policies must be approved by leadership, aligned with applicable laws and standards, and reviewed periodically to ensure they remain current. User awareness training plays a vital role in compliance, as users must understand their responsibilities regarding data access and protection. Security teams must also stay informed about changes in the regulatory landscape and adapt access control policies and systems accordingly.

Ultimately, compliance considerations in access control are not static checkboxes but ongoing responsibilities that must be woven into the organization's operational and cultural fabric. They require coordination between technical controls, policy frameworks, human behavior, and external requirements. By implementing comprehensive, auditable, and adaptable access control systems, organizations can meet their regulatory obligations while strengthening their overall security posture. The goal is not only to avoid penalties but to establish a mature access governance model that supports transparency, accountability, and trust in a digitally connected world.

Centralized Firewall Management

Centralized firewall management has become an essential strategy for organizations striving to maintain consistent security policies, reduce operational complexity, and improve visibility across increasingly distributed and hybrid network environments. As enterprises expand their infrastructures to include branch offices, cloud platforms, data centers, and mobile workforces, the traditional model of managing firewalls individually at each location becomes inefficient, error-prone, and nearly impossible to scale. Centralized management provides a unified platform from which security administrators can configure, monitor, and enforce firewall policies across all network segments. It ensures standardization of rules, enhances compliance, facilitates auditing, and enables faster response to evolving threats. With cyberattacks growing in frequency and sophistication, a fragmented firewall architecture is a liability, whereas centralization offers the cohesion necessary for robust and adaptive defense.

At the heart of centralized firewall management is the ability to define and deploy policies across multiple firewalls from a single console. This eliminates the need to manually log into each device to create or update rules, reducing the risk of configuration drift and inconsistencies that can result from human error. Instead of duplicating rules across devices, administrators create policy templates that can be applied globally or tailored for specific regions, departments, or zones. These templates allow for both macro-level governance and micro-level customization, enabling organizations to maintain a uniform security posture while addressing local operational needs. When a change is required—such as adding a new rule to block a threat or modifying access permissions—it can be pushed to all relevant devices in minutes, ensuring swift and synchronized enforcement.

Visibility is another critical benefit of centralized management. A single dashboard provides insights into firewall health, traffic flows, rule effectiveness, and threat activity across the entire infrastructure. This holistic perspective allows security teams to detect anomalies, track incidents, and analyze patterns more efficiently than if data were siloed across multiple interfaces. It also simplifies troubleshooting and performance tuning, as administrators can quickly identify which firewalls are experiencing high load, where traffic bottlenecks are forming, or whether certain rules are generating a high number of hits or denials. Logs and alerts are aggregated into a centralized repository, streamlining correlation and investigation efforts and supporting proactive threat detection and response.

Centralized management is indispensable in the context of compliance and audit readiness. Regulations such as PCI DSS, HIPAA, SOX, and GDPR require organizations to demonstrate control over their network security, including firewall configurations, access control rules, and logging practices. With a centralized system, administrators can produce detailed reports that show which rules are in place, who made changes, and when those changes occurred. Role-based access control ensures that only authorized personnel can modify policies, and audit trails record every action taken within the management platform. These capabilities not only support external audits but also internal governance, helping organizations maintain accountability and transparency in their security operations.

Scalability is a defining characteristic of centralized firewall management. As organizations grow, they can add new firewalls without significantly increasing the management burden. New devices can be onboarded through automated workflows, pulling predefined configurations and policies from the central repository. This reduces deployment time, ensures consistency, and eliminates the need to manually replicate settings. In environments with hundreds or even thousands of firewalls, such automation is essential to maintaining operational efficiency. Centralized management platforms often support hierarchical administration models, where global policies are set at the top level while local administrators are granted limited control over their assigned domains. This balance allows for centralized oversight while preserving the agility needed for local decision-making.

The integration of artificial intelligence and machine learning into centralized firewall management platforms is enhancing their capabilities further. These technologies can analyze traffic behavior, detect unusual patterns, recommend policy changes, and even automate the creation of new rules in response to emerging threats. Machine learning models can identify redundant or unused rules, suggest optimizations to reduce latency or rule evaluation time, and detect policy conflicts that might otherwise go unnoticed. As these systems learn from historical data and external threat intelligence, they become increasingly effective at anticipating threats and adjusting firewall behavior in real time. This adaptive capability is critical in a threat landscape that evolves faster than manual processes can respond.

In hybrid and multi-cloud environments, centralized firewall management becomes even more important. Organizations must secure workloads that span private data centers, public cloud services, and remote locations. Each environment may use different firewall technologies, such as virtual firewalls, cloud-native security groups, or container-based security controls. Centralized management platforms bridge these differences by abstracting policy creation from the underlying technologies. Administrators define access rules, inspection profiles, and logging requirements in a unified language, which the platform then translates into configurations compatible with each environment. This abstraction ensures consistent security policies regardless of where the workloads reside and eliminates the need to master multiple vendor-specific interfaces.

Centralized management also facilitates integration with broader security ecosystems. Firewalls do not operate in isolation; they interact with intrusion prevention systems, endpoint detection platforms, identity providers, and SIEM systems. Centralized platforms act as hubs that coordinate these interactions, sharing threat intelligence, receiving alerts, and adjusting policies dynamically in response to changing risk levels. For example, if an endpoint detection system flags a device as compromised, the firewall management system can automatically isolate the device by updating access rules. Similarly, threat intelligence feeds can trigger the creation of rules that block communication with newly identified malicious domains or IP addresses. This orchestration enhances situational awareness and ensures that firewalls contribute to a cohesive and proactive defense strategy.

One of the challenges in centralized firewall management is maintaining performance and reliability across geographically dispersed deployments. Latency, bandwidth constraints, and availability issues must be accounted for in the design of the management architecture. Solutions often include distributed collectors or agents that operate locally and synchronize with the central console, ensuring that policies are enforced even if connectivity to the management system is temporarily lost. These agents also collect logs and metrics locally, buffering data until it can be transmitted to the central system. Redundancy and failover mechanisms are essential to ensure that the management infrastructure itself does not become a single point of failure.

Training and change management are also essential to the successful implementation of centralized firewall management. Administrators must be familiar with the platform's capabilities, best practices for policy design, and procedures for change control and rollback. Organizations must establish workflows for requesting, approving, and documenting rule changes, with appropriate checks to prevent accidental disruptions or misconfigurations. Regular reviews of firewall policies, including audits of rule usage and compliance checks, help maintain the effectiveness of the system over time. User feedback, threat analysis, and performance data should inform ongoing adjustments, ensuring that the firewall infrastructure evolves in step with organizational needs and technological developments.

Centralized firewall management is more than a convenience; it is a strategic necessity in the face of growing complexity, accelerating threats, and increasing regulatory demands. By consolidating control, improving visibility, and enabling automation, centralized management empowers security teams to protect their networks with precision and agility. It transforms firewall operations from a fragmented and reactive task into a coordinated and proactive discipline, aligned with the broader goals of security, compliance, and business continuity. As digital transformation continues to redefine enterprise architecture, centralized firewall management will remain a cornerstone of resilient and intelligent cybersecurity operations.

Using APIs to Manage Firewall Rules

Using APIs to manage firewall rules has revolutionized the way network security policies are deployed, modified, and maintained across modern IT environments. In the past, managing firewalls involved manual configuration through command-line interfaces or graphical user interfaces, which was both time-consuming and prone to human error. As networks have become more dynamic and distributed, this traditional model has proven to be inadequate for organizations that demand agility, consistency, and scalability in their security operations. Application Programming Interfaces, or APIs, provide a programmatic interface to firewall systems, allowing administrators and automated systems to interact with firewall configurations in a consistent, repeatable, and efficient manner. By leveraging APIs, organizations can integrate firewall rule management into broader automation workflows, continuous deployment pipelines, and infrastructure-as-code frameworks.

APIs expose the configuration and control functionalities of firewalls in a structured format, typically using RESTful interfaces with standard HTTP methods such as GET, POST, PUT, and DELETE. These methods correspond to actions like retrieving current rules, creating new policies, updating existing ones, or deleting obsolete entries. Instead of logging into each firewall individually, administrators can write scripts or use automation platforms to issue API calls that manage rules across multiple devices simultaneously. This centralized and automated approach significantly reduces the overhead involved in rule management, especially in environments where firewalls must be updated frequently to reflect changes in applications, users, or security policies. It also reduces the risk of inconsistencies that can arise from manual processes, ensuring that policies are applied uniformly and in compliance with governance standards.

The integration of firewall management APIs with configuration management tools such as Ansible, Terraform, and Puppet enables security teams to treat firewall rules as code. This practice, often referred to as policy-as-code, allows teams to define rules in structured formats like JSON or YAML, store them in version-controlled repositories, and deploy them through automated pipelines. Changes to firewall policies can be tracked, reviewed, and rolled back just like software code, introducing a level of transparency and control that was previously difficult to achieve. Policy-as-code also supports collaboration between security, operations, and development teams, aligning security enforcement with agile and DevOps practices. In dynamic cloud environments where virtual machines, containers, and services are constantly created and destroyed, API-driven rule management ensures that security policies can keep pace without introducing bottlenecks.

Another benefit of using APIs for firewall rule management is the ability to integrate with external data sources and systems. Threat intelligence feeds, vulnerability scanners, identity providers, and security information and event management platforms can all contribute context to rule creation and modification. For example, if a threat intelligence platform identifies a new malicious IP address, it can trigger an API call that adds a deny rule to block traffic from that source across all relevant firewalls. Similarly, if a vulnerability scanner detects a critical flaw in a public-facing application, an automation script can use the firewall API to temporarily restrict access until the issue is resolved. This level of integration allows for real-time, intelligence-driven adjustments to firewall policies, reducing the window of exposure and enabling faster incident response.

Monitoring and auditing are also enhanced through API usage. Firewalls that support APIs typically provide endpoints for retrieving logs, metrics, and status information. These data can be consumed by monitoring tools or fed into centralized dashboards for real-time visibility into rule effectiveness, rule hit counts, policy changes, and system health. Administrators can query the API to determine which rules are being used, which are obsolete, and which may be conflicting or redundant. This information supports policy optimization and ensures that the rule base remains lean, relevant, and efficient. Regular audits of firewall rules, often required for compliance, become easier when data can be retrieved programmatically and analyzed using standardized tools.

Security is a critical consideration when using APIs for firewall management. Because APIs provide powerful control over network security, they must be protected against unauthorized access and abuse. Strong authentication methods such as API keys, OAuth tokens, or certificate-based access must be enforced. Role-based access control should restrict what actions different users or systems can perform via the API, ensuring that only authorized personnel can modify rules or access sensitive data. All API traffic should be encrypted using TLS to protect it from interception. Logging and monitoring of API calls are also essential to detect and investigate suspicious activities. By enforcing rigorous security controls, organizations can safely leverage the flexibility of APIs without compromising the integrity of their firewall infrastructure.

Scalability is another area where APIs excel. As organizations expand their networks to include multiple firewalls across different regions, data centers, and cloud environments, managing rules manually becomes impractical. APIs make it possible to scale firewall rule management to thousands of devices without adding proportional overhead. Scripts and orchestration tools can issue API calls in parallel, update configurations based on templates, and validate rule application automatically. This scalability is crucial for large enterprises, service providers, and cloud-native organizations that require consistent and rapid policy enforcement across diverse and growing infrastructures.

Change management and governance processes also benefit from API-driven firewall rule management. By integrating API calls into change request workflows, organizations can ensure that all rule changes are tracked, approved, and documented. Integration with IT service management platforms allows requests to be submitted, validated, and fulfilled through structured processes, with audit trails capturing who requested the change, who approved it, and what actions were taken. This level of governance not only supports internal accountability but also helps organizations meet external compliance requirements related to access control and change management.

The future of firewall management is increasingly API-driven, aligning with broader trends toward automation, infrastructure as code, and intelligent security orchestration. Vendors are continually enhancing their API offerings, adding support for more granular control, real-time telemetry, and integration with artificial intelligence and machine learning tools. As APIs become more powerful and accessible, the potential for innovation in firewall rule management grows. Organizations can build custom interfaces, self-service portals, and automated response systems that leverage firewall APIs to enforce security policies with unprecedented speed and precision.

Using APIs to manage firewall rules is no longer a novelty but a necessity in modern, agile, and cloud-connected environments. It empowers security teams to respond faster, operate more efficiently, and maintain greater control over their network defenses. By integrating firewall management into automated workflows, aligning it with code-based practices, and connecting it to broader security and operational systems, APIs unlock a new level of capability and resilience. The shift toward API-based management reflects a deeper transformation in how security is conceived and executed, moving from static, reactive models to dynamic, integrated, and proactive architectures that are better suited to the demands of today's digital world.

Logging, Auditing, and Reporting

Logging, auditing, and reporting are foundational components of any comprehensive security architecture, especially within the domain of firewall and access control management. These practices are not only vital for detecting and responding to security incidents, but they also support accountability, regulatory compliance, operational visibility, and long-term security posture improvement. As networks grow more complex and threats become more sophisticated, the need to understand exactly what is happening within an environment in real time and retrospectively has never been more critical. Logging provides the raw data that captures every action, event, and anomaly. Auditing ensures that these records are reviewed, validated, and used to enforce policies and standards. Reporting translates this information into actionable insights for both technical teams and executive leadership.

At its core, logging is the process by which firewalls and other network devices record events such as allowed and denied connections, configuration changes, user logins, rule hits, packet drops, and system errors. Every piece of traffic that passes through a firewall can be logged, and this creates a granular record of what occurred, when, where, and under what circumstances. For example, a denied connection from an unauthorized IP address attempting to access a protected service can be logged with details about the source IP, destination port, protocol used, and time of the attempt. This log entry becomes invaluable during an investigation into a potential intrusion or policy violation. Logging can also include more detailed contextual information such as application identifiers, user IDs, session IDs, and geolocation data, all of which help security analysts understand the full scope of an event.

The effectiveness of logging depends on the structure and completeness of the log data. Logs should be timestamped using a synchronized and trusted time source to support correlation across systems. Each log entry should follow a standardized format that makes it easy to parse, search, and analyze. Modern firewalls support exporting logs in formats compatible with syslog servers, log aggregators, and security information and event management systems. These systems collect logs from multiple sources across the infrastructure, normalize the data, and store it for long-term retention. Because logging can generate enormous volumes of data, especially in high-traffic environments, organizations must implement strategies for filtering, compressing, and archiving logs efficiently without losing critical information.

Auditing is the practice of systematically reviewing log data and system configurations to verify compliance with internal policies, external regulations, and industry best practices. It involves identifying anomalies, inconsistencies, and potential violations by comparing observed behavior with expected norms. For example, an audit might reveal that certain firewall rules are not being hit, indicating that they are obsolete or misconfigured. It might also uncover cases where administrative changes were made without proper authorization, pointing to a breakdown in change control processes. Auditing also includes evaluating the completeness of logs, checking for gaps or missing data that could indicate tampering or misconfiguration. Regular audits help maintain the integrity of the logging infrastructure and ensure that security controls are being applied and enforced as intended.

Security audits also assess the effectiveness of access controls, ensuring that users and systems are only granted the privileges they need. Logs can be used to verify that access attempts conform to assigned permissions and to detect any instances of privilege escalation or unauthorized access. In highly regulated environments, audits must be thorough and well-documented to demonstrate compliance with frameworks such as GDPR, HIPAA, PCI-DSS, SOX, or ISO 27001. These audits often require organizations to show not just that they have logging in place, but that they actively monitor and respond to log data, that they have conducted access reviews, and that any anomalies are followed up with documented investigations and remediations.

Reporting is the process by which the results of logging and auditing activities are communicated to stakeholders. Reports can be technical, operational, or executive in nature, each serving a different audience and purpose. Technical reports might detail firewall rule usage, intrusion attempts, or traffic patterns. Operational reports could focus on system uptime, configuration changes, or user activity. Executive reports distill this information into trends, risks, compliance status, and recommendations for action. Automated reporting tools allow security teams to generate and distribute these insights on a regular schedule, ensuring that leadership stays informed and that decisions are based on data.

Effective reporting requires that the underlying data be accurate, timely, and presented in a format that aligns with the needs of the audience. Dashboards and visualizations can enhance understanding by highlighting key metrics, outliers, and changes over time. Reports that show spikes in denied traffic, unusual patterns of outbound connections, or changes in user behavior can prompt further investigation or immediate response. Reports can also be used to demonstrate return on investment for security controls, showing how many threats were detected and blocked, how quickly incidents were resolved, and how risk exposure has been reduced over time.

Another critical role of reporting is in incident response. When a security incident occurs, investigators rely heavily on logs to understand the timeline of events, identify affected systems, and determine the method of attack. Reports generated from log data can help reconstruct the attack path, identify indicators of compromise, and support attribution efforts. In many cases, regulators or law enforcement agencies will require these reports as part of post-incident investigations. The quality and completeness of log data and the ability to quickly generate accurate reports can significantly influence the effectiveness of the response and the organization's credibility in the aftermath.

The implementation of logging, auditing, and reporting must be supported by a clear policy that defines what data should be logged, how long it should be retained, who has access to it, and how it should be protected. Logs contain sensitive information and must be stored securely, with access limited to authorized personnel. Organizations must also plan for log storage capacity, ensuring that logs are retained long enough to support investigations and compliance but are eventually archived or purged in accordance with data retention policies. Backup and redundancy for log storage systems must be in place to prevent data loss in the event of hardware failure or disaster.

As cybersecurity threats continue to evolve and regulatory demands increase, logging, auditing, and reporting will remain indispensable tools for managing and securing modern networks. They provide the foundation for visibility, accountability, and continuous improvement. By investing in robust logging infrastructures, conducting thorough audits, and generating insightful reports, organizations equip themselves to detect threats early, respond effectively, and demonstrate that they are meeting their obligations to protect systems, data, and users. These processes transform raw data into strategic intelligence, turning passive information into active defense mechanisms that support resilient and trustworthy operations.

Future Trends in Access Control and Filtering

The future of access control and filtering is being shaped by the rapid evolution of technology, the decentralization of infrastructure, and the increasingly complex threat landscape. Traditional models of perimeter-based security and static access control are giving way to dynamic, adaptive systems that prioritize context, behavior, and identity over location or fixed credentials. As enterprises embrace hybrid cloud environments, remote work, Internet of Things devices, and artificial intelligence, the mechanisms for controlling access and filtering network traffic must become more intelligent, automated, and integrated. These future trends are not just incremental improvements but represent a fundamental shift in how security is architected and enforced across digital ecosystems.

One of the most significant trends is the continued rise of zero trust architecture. In a zero trust model, no user or device is automatically trusted, regardless of its location within or outside the corporate network. Access is granted only after verifying a combination of factors, including user identity, device health, geolocation, time of access, and behavioral patterns. This shift requires access control systems to move away from simple IP-based rules toward policies that are dynamic, risk-based, and continuously evaluated. Access decisions are no longer static checkpoints but ongoing assessments that adapt to changing context. Zero trust principles demand filtering systems that can enforce granular controls at every point in the network, including endpoints, cloud services, and internal microsegments.

Another key trend is the growing role of artificial intelligence and machine learning in access control and filtering. Traditional systems rely heavily on predefined rules and signature-based detection, which can struggle to keep up with novel attack vectors or subtle misuse. AI-driven systems can analyze large volumes of data to detect anomalies, learn normal usage patterns, and predict potential threats before they fully manifest. In access control, this means identifying behavior that deviates from the baseline for a given user or role and triggering step-up authentication, restricted access, or alerts. In filtering, it allows real-time identification of malicious traffic, even if it uses encryption or obfuscation techniques. As AI models become more accurate and adaptive, they will play a larger role in automating security decisions and reducing the burden on human administrators.

Identity is becoming the new perimeter in access control. As organizations adopt cloud-first and remote-first strategies, the traditional network edge becomes irrelevant. What matters is not where a request comes from but who is making the request and under what conditions. Federated identity systems, single sign-on, and multi-factor authentication are being combined with contextual access policies that assess device compliance, recent activity, and even biometric data. Identity-based filtering allows organizations to apply differentiated controls based on user roles and responsibilities, enabling the principle of least privilege at scale. This trend is also expanding into machine and application identities, ensuring that services can authenticate and authorize each other securely in automated environments.

Access control and filtering are also becoming more tightly integrated with DevOps and infrastructure-as-code practices. Security policies are being written and maintained in code, stored in version-controlled repositories, and deployed alongside application updates. This enables faster, more consistent enforcement and ensures that access rules evolve in tandem with the systems they protect. Policy-as-code frameworks support automated testing, rollback, and auditing, reducing the risk of human error and supporting compliance. As organizations adopt continuous integration and continuous deployment pipelines, the ability to automate security policy enforcement becomes essential for maintaining both speed and security. In the future, access control will be embedded directly into the development lifecycle, with security teams collaborating with developers to define and enforce rules early in the process.

Decentralization and edge computing are driving the need for distributed access control and filtering capabilities. As data and compute resources move closer to users and devices, centralized enforcement becomes impractical. Future systems must be able to enforce policies locally, even in the absence of constant connectivity to central controllers. Lightweight filtering agents and access enforcement points will be embedded in devices, gateways, and edge servers, operating autonomously while synchronizing with cloud-based policy engines when connectivity is available. This approach ensures that security is maintained even in disconnected or low-latency environments, such as manufacturing plants, remote facilities, or autonomous vehicles.

Encryption is becoming ubiquitous across network traffic, creating challenges for traditional filtering methods that rely on visibility into payloads. To address this, future filtering systems will need to support selective decryption, encrypted traffic analytics, and endpoint-based inspection. Rather than breaking and inspecting all encrypted traffic, intelligent systems will identify suspicious flows based on metadata, traffic patterns, and behavioral cues. Additionally, endpoint security solutions will play a larger role in inspecting data before it is encrypted or after it is decrypted at the application layer. Collaboration between network and endpoint security tools will be essential for maintaining visibility and control in an encrypted world.

The proliferation of devices and the expansion of the Internet of Things introduce unique access control challenges. Many IoT devices lack robust security controls and cannot support traditional authentication or filtering mechanisms. Future systems will need to identify devices based on behavior, firmware fingerprints, or passive network observations and enforce policies accordingly. Microsegmentation and device quarantine features will become more common, isolating potentially vulnerable devices while still allowing them to perform their functions. Access policies will need to account for device type, purpose, and risk profile, ensuring that even unmanaged or legacy devices can be integrated securely into the network.

Human-centric design will also influence the evolution of access control and filtering. Security systems must become more intuitive, minimizing friction for legitimate users while maintaining robust protections. Adaptive authentication, contextual prompts, and user behavior analytics will allow security measures to operate silently in the background, only surfacing when risk is detected. In filtering, false positives and unnecessary blocks can erode user trust and productivity, so systems must be tuned to minimize disruptions while remaining effective. Usability will become a core metric for evaluating the success of security systems, with organizations striving to strike a balance between protection and accessibility.

Regulatory and compliance demands will continue to shape the future of access control and filtering. As data protection laws evolve and expand globally, organizations will need to demonstrate not just that controls are in place, but that they are effective, auditable, and aligned with evolving standards. Future systems will include built-in compliance reporting, automated policy validation, and integration with governance platforms. Security policies will be mapped to regulatory requirements, and deviations will be detected and remediated automatically. This trend reflects the growing intersection of security, privacy, and accountability, requiring a unified approach that combines technology, policy, and process.

As access control and filtering become more intelligent, distributed, and integrated, the role of the security professional will also evolve. Rather than configuring rules manually, security teams will define intent, set strategic objectives, and oversee automated systems that enforce policies across the environment. The focus will shift from reactive configuration to proactive governance, from troubleshooting individual issues to orchestrating complex security ecosystems. Education, adaptability, and collaboration will be essential skills, as the boundaries between security, IT, and development continue to blur. The future of access control and filtering will be defined not only by the capabilities of the technology but by the ability of organizations to adapt, innovate, and lead in a world where security is no longer optional but embedded in every layer of the digital experience.

Case Studies in Firewalling

Examining real-world case studies in firewalling provides valuable insights into how different organizations implement, manage, and adapt their firewall strategies to meet the challenges of evolving threats, complex infrastructures, and regulatory demands. Each deployment presents unique technical, organizational, and environmental variables that shape how firewalls are configured and integrated into broader security postures. These cases not only illustrate best practices and common pitfalls but also demonstrate the practical impact of firewalling decisions on business continuity, performance, and security outcomes.

In one large-scale enterprise deployment, a global financial services company with offices across five continents undertook a firewall consolidation project aimed at improving security visibility and simplifying rule management. Previously, each regional office operated with independently managed firewalls, leading to inconsistencies in policy enforcement, duplicated rules, and difficulty auditing configurations. The company chose to adopt a centralized firewall management solution that allowed them to define global policies while delegating limited administrative access to local teams. The transition required careful planning to merge thousands of rules across different platforms. During the migration phase, redundant rules were identified using automated analysis tools, and policy conflicts were resolved by creating a master template. Once implemented, the organization significantly reduced the number of active rules and gained real-time visibility into all firewall activity from a centralized dashboard. The project also included the introduction of role-based access controls and automated change tracking, which improved compliance with financial industry regulations. The company reported faster incident response times and a marked decrease in unauthorized access attempts.

Another case involved a mid-sized manufacturing company that suffered a ransomware attack that originated from an exposed remote desktop protocol port. Although their perimeter firewall had been configured to block most inbound traffic, an exception had been created temporarily for a third-party vendor and was never removed. This oversight allowed the attacker to exploit the open port using stolen credentials. Following the incident, the company conducted a forensic review and discovered that firewall logs had not been actively monitored, and no alerting system was in place for unusual access patterns. The recovery process included a complete overhaul of their firewall strategy. They implemented strict access controls, closed all unnecessary ports, and adopted a policy of least privilege for remote access. Additionally, they integrated their firewall logs with a SIEM platform to enable continuous monitoring and alerting. The company also began conducting quarterly firewall audits and created a formal process for reviewing and expiring temporary rules. As a result, they significantly hardened their network perimeter and improved their resilience against similar attacks.

A government agency managing critical infrastructure offers another illustrative case. The agency faced the challenge of segmenting its operational technology network from its IT network without disrupting essential services. Firewalls were deployed at the boundary between the two networks, with strict rules governing traffic direction and type. Given the sensitivity of the systems involved, the firewall had to support deep packet inspection and intrusion prevention capabilities. The agency also required logging to be immutable and retained for several years in accordance with national cybersecurity regulations. To meet these requirements, they implemented high-availability firewalls in active-passive pairs with redundant connections. A policy of deny-by-default was applied, and only explicitly allowed traffic was permitted. Application-layer inspection was used to detect unauthorized protocol usage that might otherwise bypass traditional port-based rules. The deployment was accompanied by a robust change management framework and coordination with operational staff to test rule changes before deployment. Over time, the agency observed a decrease in anomalous activity at the boundary, and audits confirmed improved compliance with critical infrastructure protection standards.

In a different scenario, a fast-growing technology startup focused on rapid deployment of services found itself facing scalability issues with its firewall infrastructure. As the company scaled up its cloud-based services, the existing firewall model, which relied on manually defined static rules, could not keep pace with the frequent changes in microservice instances and dynamic IP addressing. To solve this problem, the security team transitioned to a cloud-native firewalling model using security groups and service tags that could automatically adjust based on the context and identity of workloads. Instead of managing IPs and ports manually, policies were written to reference application names and roles. Integration with the cloud provider's identity and access management system allowed firewall rules to follow services wherever they were deployed, even across regions. Additionally, the team employed infrastructure-as-code to define and manage firewall rules, ensuring consistency across development, staging, and production environments. This automation drastically reduced configuration errors and accelerated security reviews. The company achieved a more agile and scalable security posture without compromising visibility or control.

An educational institution presents another compelling example, where the firewall strategy had to accommodate thousands of users, including students, faculty, and guest devices, across a sprawling campus with multiple buildings and internet connections. The institution adopted a zone-based firewalling approach, segmenting the network into logical areas such as administration, faculty, student housing, research labs, and public access. Each zone was governed by specific policies reflecting its risk profile and usage requirements. To manage high volumes of traffic and ensure availability during peak usage periods, the institution deployed firewalls with load balancing and failover capabilities. Special attention was given to protecting the research zones, which contained sensitive data and intellectual property. Multi-layer inspection and strict outbound filtering were implemented to prevent data exfiltration. The university also used time-based access control for certain facilities, disabling access outside of designated hours to reduce exposure. Regular training for IT staff and policy review sessions were part of the strategy to ensure the firewall rules remained aligned with changing needs and technology updates.

Each of these cases underscores the importance of aligning firewall strategy with organizational goals, threat models, and operational realities. Whether centralizing control in a multinational enterprise, recovering from a breach in a smaller company, protecting critical infrastructure, enabling scalability in the cloud, or securing diverse academic environments, the role of the firewall is essential but must be supported by proper planning, policy enforcement, and integration with the broader security ecosystem. Firewalls are not standalone solutions; they are dynamic components of a larger architecture that includes identity management, monitoring, automation, and governance. Through real-world application and continuous improvement, firewalling remains a cornerstone of effective cybersecurity strategy in every sector.

Summary and Final Thoughts

The domains of firewalling, access control, zoning, and context-based filtering have become more critical than ever as digital infrastructure continues to evolve. Throughout this exploration of firewall technologies and traffic control mechanisms, a central theme emerges: security is no longer static. It is a living, adaptive, and integrated aspect of every system, application, and connection. The traditional view of firewalls as simple packet filters has been thoroughly transformed. Modern firewalls are intelligent, policy-driven systems that operate at multiple layers of the network stack, capable of deep inspection, user-aware access control, dynamic policy enforcement, and real-time threat prevention. Their role extends well beyond the perimeter, becoming intrinsic to both the architecture and the operational fabric of secure computing environments.

Access control has equally advanced from simple username and password combinations or basic IP filtering into a nuanced, multi-dimensional discipline. Identity, role, device posture, geographic location, time of access, and behavioral analytics all play a role in determining who should have access to what, when, and under what conditions. The principle of least privilege is reinforced not through static configurations, but through dynamic evaluation and automated enforcement. Systems now must make real-time decisions based on changing inputs, constantly re-evaluating trust and adapting permissions accordingly. This adaptive access control reflects the shift in security thinking from network-centric models to identity-centric and context-aware strategies.

Zoning architectures have proven to be essential in organizing networks into segments that reflect business needs, risk tolerance, and compliance obligations. By grouping systems and users into logical zones, administrators can apply appropriate controls at the boundaries and within the segments themselves. Zone policies are not simply walls; they are tailored filters that enable secure interaction between departments, services, and users while preventing unauthorized or unnecessary movement. These architectures support not only operational efficiency but also incident containment and threat isolation. When well designed, zoning reduces complexity and improves the overall resilience of the network.

Context-based filtering, including mechanisms like CBAC and next-generation firewalls, enables granular inspection of traffic that goes far beyond matching IP addresses and ports. These tools can analyze the state of connections, the content of communications, and the behavior of users and applications. They are capable of detecting anomalies, blocking threats in real time, and applying policies that evolve as situations change. This capability is especially crucial in an environment where attackers are skilled at disguising malicious traffic as legitimate communication. Modern threats do not always follow predictable patterns, and the ability to understand the context of activity is indispensable for accurate detection and effective defense.

Throughout this body of work, the emphasis has been placed on how various components interlock. Firewalls are not isolated devices. They are integrated with identity systems, orchestration tools, threat intelligence platforms, and monitoring solutions. This ecosystem of interoperability is necessary because the scope and scale of modern infrastructure demand automation, intelligence, and coordination. In hybrid cloud, multi-cloud, and edge environments, consistency and control can only be achieved through centralized management systems, APIs, and policy-as-code methodologies. These integrations ensure that policies are applied accurately, that enforcement remains effective despite environmental complexity, and that changes can be made quickly in response to emerging risks.

Equally important is the human aspect of firewalling and traffic control. Designing effective rules, implementing zoning strategies, managing exceptions, auditing configurations, and responding to incidents all require informed and trained professionals. The tools have become more sophisticated, but they still rely on security practitioners to make decisions, interpret data, and align technical controls with organizational goals. Security culture, training programs, and communication between teams are as vital as any piece of technology. Mistakes in configuration, failures to monitor logs, or lapses in policy enforcement can render even the most advanced systems ineffective. Therefore, fostering a proactive, well-informed security team is a foundational element of success.

Regulatory and compliance frameworks have added further complexity to the role of firewalls and access control mechanisms. Organizations are expected to maintain not only security but also traceability, transparency, and accountability. Policies must be auditable, logs must be retained and analyzed, and access decisions must be defensible. As regulations continue to evolve globally, organizations must stay vigilant in aligning their firewall strategies with both the letter and spirit of these requirements. The ability to demonstrate compliance, generate reports, and prove that controls are functioning as intended is now a core responsibility of any firewall deployment.

Looking ahead, the field of firewalling and traffic control will continue to evolve rapidly. Threats will become more automated, more personalized, and more persistent. Cloud-native architectures, AI-driven applications, and decentralized computing models will demand ever more flexible and responsive security solutions. Firewalls will need to evolve from gatekeepers to intelligent participants in a broader security fabric that includes real-time threat detection, automated response, and adaptive risk management. The lines between firewall, intrusion detection, access control, and monitoring will blur further, giving rise to unified platforms that perform multiple roles with greater accuracy and less manual effort.

At the same time, the core principles will remain. Protect what matters. Know who is accessing what. Enforce policies consistently. Monitor for deviations. Respond to threats decisively. These timeless objectives continue to guide the implementation and evolution of security systems, regardless of how the technology changes. The success of any firewalling or access control strategy depends on understanding the environment, defining clear objectives, and implementing controls that are aligned, intelligent, and operationally sustainable.

This comprehensive journey through firewalling, zoning, access control lists, and context-based filtering underscores the strategic importance of traffic control in securing digital environments. These components, when thoughtfully designed and effectively managed, enable organizations to operate confidently in a world of constant change and relentless threats. They support not just defense, but trust, enabling innovation, growth, and resilience. As security continues to move from the edge into the core of infrastructure, governance, and business strategy, firewalling and traffic control will remain indispensable instruments of order in an increasingly complex and connected world.

www.ingramcontent.com/pod-product-compliance
Lightning Source LLC
LaVergne TN
LVHW051236050326
832903LV00028B/2429